None of the Above:
Why Non-Voters Are America's Political Majority

None of the Above:
Why Non-Voters Are America's Political Majority

By Sy Leon

Fox & Wilkes
San Francisco

First Edition 1976
Second Edition (revised) 1996
© 1996 by Sy Leon

All rights reserved, including the right to reproduce this book or portions thereof in any form, without permission in writing from the publisher.

This edition published by Fox & Wilkes
938 Howard Street, Suite 202
San Francisco, CA 94103

ISBN: 0-930073-17-7

Cover Design: Chris Van Vleit
Composition and Layout: Carol Olmstead

Manufactured in the United States of America

☑ *None of the Above*

Contents

Preface vii
Introduction to the 1996 Edition
            By John A. Pugsley 1
Chapter 1: "The Vanishing Voter: A Look at
            Non-Voting as a Purposive Act"
            By V. Lance Tarrance 13
Chapter 2: None of the Above Is Acceptable ... 23
Chapter 3: The Lesser of Two Evils 30
Chapter 4: Politicalese — The Language of
            Deceit 35
Chapter 5: "The Good Of Society" 42
Chapter 6: Where The Individual Vote Really
            Counts 48
Chapter 7: The Political Mystique 57
Chapter 8: The World's Oldest Profession 64
Chapter 9: Principles Are Practical 73
Chapter 10: What Is Your Freedom Worth? 79
Chapter 11: Freedom In The Balance 87
Chapter 12: A Gang By Any Other Name 93
Chapter 13: Are Non-Voters Apathetic? 100
Chapter 14: Choice: The Third Alternative 107
Chapter 15: Order and Chaos 114
Chapter 16: Political Conflict of Interest 120
Chapter 17: Performance Bonding Of Politicians;
            Campaign Promise Insurance 125

v

☑ *None of the Above*

Chapter 18: Politicoholism: An Epidemic Of National Concern 131
Chapter 19: The Politician Is Best Who Works Least 138
Chapter 20: Unethical Employment: The Social And Personal Consequences Of the Profession Of Politics 145
Chapter 21: Between The Lights 151
Chapter 22: Everything Works 158
Chapter 23: To Go Forward, Put Your Mind In Gear 165
Chapter 24: Gadfly At The Post Office 171
Chapter 25: Optimism or Pessimism? 178
Chapter 26: How To Achieve And Maintain Your Freedom Through Political Actions And Other Forms Of Violence 185
About the Author 191

☑ *None of the Above*

Preface

Who is this fellow? And what makes him think that he knows all the answers?

I expect those two questions to be posed by many who read this book and consider the observations in it. I think it will be helpful to you, the reader, to know something of my background and why I choose to involve myself with such radical views.

It's my nature to be inquisitive and skeptical. I have always been intrigued with people — their motivation, diversity, and actions. I completed my formal schooling with a lackluster attempt at college. I was attracted to the business world and because of my interest in people and a desire for independence and money, spent most of my time in sales and marketing. It wasn't until I'd reached my late thirties that I became deeply interested in the study of philosophy and economics and, consequently, psychology. After several years of concentrated self-directed study and several specialized courses, I joined the staff of Rampart College, then located in Colorado, as an instructor.

Rampart was a small, private education project founded and run by Robert LeFevre. The opportunity to work and study with LeFevre was the most significant influence on the research, learn-

☑ *None of the Above*

ing, development and integration leading to my present views. It has been said that we stand on the shoulders of our predecessors and teachers; I believe this to be true. And although my ideas are my responsibility alone, LeFevre's shoulders have provided me with a very broad and firm base. In my 10 years at Rampart College as an instructor, director, and finally president, I was privileged to discuss and study with many professors, writers, and businessmen and women. As a result of these years of exposure to intense, stimulating ideas and people, I have formed the views expounded in this book.

While each of us is a unique human being with his or her* own characteristics, values, goals, desires and so on, there are some qualities which we have in common — just because we *are* human beings. One of those qualities seems to be a common view that we want to live in a rich society which is relatively peaceful and allows maximum opportunities for every person to satisfy his own unique desires and goals.

At the risk of oversimplifying a problem of enormous complexity, I will say that this question — how to accommodate the common, or social,

---

* For ease of communication, the term "he" is used in the balance of the text to mean "he or she" (and "his" to mean "his or hers," etc.)—to do otherwise proves cumbersome and detracts from both the form and content.

☑ *None of the Above*

environment to individual human wants and goals — has been so profoundly confusing that it is the root cause of virtually all social discontent.

Let me state at this point that I'm not suggesting that this book and these ideas hold the answer. If anything, it may raise still more questions in recognizing that for several thousand years human beings have failed to achieve a way to live alongside each other without a basic view that they will rely ultimately on some means of violence to settle disagreements.

In technological fields, the mind of man has made fantastic accomplishments, and the future is bright and glowing with anticipation of still greater scientific progress. But in the area of human interaction — social interchange — we are still employing the same ideas that were in vogue when "society" consisted of roving bands of savages. Yes, technologically we are brilliant and about to break into the twenty-first century in a noble and proud manner; but psychologically and sociologically we have yet to emerge from pre-Biblical times.

Could it be that one of the key factors in this disparity is attitude? I think so. The scientist has the attitude that everything is open to question and challenge. He builds upon prior knowledge, but is always ready to consider evidence that previously established "truth" may be in error. This is

[handwritten note: Clearly not true in general. Consider how the fraud of evolution continues to promulgated by "scientists" in total disregard to facts and common sense!]

☑ *None of the Above*

the cornerstone of promise and progress; to be willing to examine, to consider, and when necessary, to correct.

I hope this book will be considered as it is intended: an effort to examine previously held opinions and assist in an assessment of what we are doing socially, collectively; to measure our ideas, values and efforts to see if they are consistent with our goals. I tend to employ light humor and satire in dealing with very serious subjects. It happens to be the way I think and the way I talk; it is not meant to be frivolous. But I believe it is an effective way to get ideas across in areas that can be very threatening to some people.

Often I'm asked about my own political affiliation or identity. My activities have been called "conservative conspiracies" by liberals, and "liberal conspiracies" by conservatives. I've been labeled as everything on the political spectrum at one time or another, from pacifist and anarchist to communist and plain old crackpot. My business card refers to me as an "anti-politician."

Actually, I'm apolitical. I have no personal interest nor desire to participate in politics...for reasons which will become evident as you read this book. The question that next arises, then, is why do I write about politics? — and that deserves an answer.

☑ *None of the Above*

All of us have personal lives and social (societal) lives. In our personal lives we can be highly selective and effect a higher degree of integrity between our values and how we express them. Our social lives are subject to greater influence from others, by necessity.

I recognize that present society will continue to rely on political methods. If I can exert some influence on the use of these methods and thereby cause some decrease in the adverse effects on my life and the lives of my neighbors, it is consistent with my personal views to make that effort. But for myself, I must make that effort from *outside* the political arena, because if I became active politically I would then become a part of the problem. And from a tactical viewpoint, it's my belief that significant political changes take place as a result of activity outside of politics rather than inside. So, ethically, I will not participate — and pragmatically, I believe it is more effective to remain an outsider.

There are many, of course, who will disagree with my reasoning — but that's not the point. I have simply tried to explain why *I* do what *I* do. I'm not saying anyone else should do the same.

To return to importance of attitude: <u>Things change when we are dissatisfied with present conditions and when we acknowledge the existence of methods for improving them.</u> To be un-

☑ *None of the Above*

happy with how things are and yet believe that nothing can be done to change them leads to frustration and disaster.

But to view the current state of affairs and take its measure realistically is healthy. To be ready and able to create new alternatives requires a positive mental attitude.

I believe that many people today have advanced psychologically and emotionally to the point where they want to exercise more control over their own lives. Conversely, there are many people who want more control over the lives of others. For the latter group, there are six thousand years of history and countless volumes of reference from Machiavelli to Hitler. But for those who want only to have more control over their own lives, I hope this book will be useful, interesting and inspiring.

— Sy Leon
December 1995

☑ *None of the Above*

LEON'S LAW OF GOVERNMENT

The amount of government control will always increase to the level of toleration of the people.

An extremely tolerant populace will suffer a dictatorship. *rule by one*

A moderately tolerant public will condone a democracy. *rule by mob*

An intolerant society will be free. *rule by law*

☑ *None of the Above*

Introduction to the 1996 Edition

by John A. Pugsley

It's hard to believe that twenty years have passed since the publication of the first edition of this book. It's not hard to believe that the book is every bit as important and timely today as it was in 1976.

The goal of all individuals of goodwill today and for most of history is and has been individual liberty — the opportunity to work where we want, keep what we earn and pursue the activities we enjoy. The brightest minds of every generation in almost all nations in recorded history have searched for the path to that goal. The discovery of how to achieve freedom has been, and is, mankind's most important quest.

Mankind has clearly failed. Nowhere on earth does man live in anything approaching freedom. Even in the United States, supposedly the "land of the free," the erosion of individual rights has become endemic. The power of the state to tax, regulate and control the lives of citizens seems to constantly grow.

☑ *None of the Above*

Freedom is the goal, yet after thousands of years of recorded history and thousands upon thousands of tries at creating systems of government that might achieve freedom for individuals, the goal has not been reached.

Why?

It has failed because those searching for a social technology that would ensure individual freedom have incorrectly assumed that freedom could only exist if we first designed the perfect form of government. Even those enlightened geniuses whom we call our "founding fathers" started from the premise that a society can only function if individuals subordinate themselves to a political authority. Outside of a relative handful of libertarians in the world, this belief that men cannot live in harmony without government is nearly universal.

[margin note: Proper gov'n't is God ordained.]

A growing number of individuals are beginning to recognize the wolf in grandmother's nightgown. Government the protector always becomes government the aggressor. Today, thinking people are becoming aware that each time grandmother kisses them, they wind up with a nasty bite. As government grows, the victims multiply.

The common issue facing all freedom-seeking individuals is, how can the cancerous growth of the state be stopped? What can we as individuals do to reverse the trend toward omnipotent gov-

☑ *None of the Above*

ernment and ultimately achieve the maximum degree of individual freedom?

The two common strategies used down through history to fight back against oppressive government have been either to overthrow tyrants by violent revolution, or to oust them through the democratic process of voting. Unfortunately, violent revolution in most cases replaces one group of tyrants with another, leaving individuals still dominated by government.

The other strategy is to use the electoral process to take control of the state. Those who choose this strategy believe that through voter education, political campaigning and the voting booth, political power can be wrested from special interests, spend-thrift politicians can be excised from government, and the state can be subdued. However, the evidence of history suggests that changing governments in the voting booth has only a modestly better short-term record than violent revolution, and in the long run, individuals are still dominated by oppressive government.

In most people's minds, revolution and voting are the only options for achieving freedom. They are wrong. There is another strategy. Unfortunately, it is so contrary to our cultural indoctrination that only a few in society have the courage to consider it, let alone to stand up against popular opinion and argue its case. This strategy rests on

☑ *None of the Above*

the premise that no other individual, whether that person elects himself by force, or pretends to have authority over you because the majority of your neighbors appointed him, has the right or justification to control your life or property.

It is my belief that a social compact in which each and every individual is free to control his life and property is the only system that can survive in perpetuity. By definition, this means a social system that abandons the right of the majority or the minority to rule. It is a system of self-rule and individual sovereignty.

Those who believe in the principle that the individual should be sovereign refuse to condone political action even as a means to an end. They reject all forms of it. They do not campaign for or against candidates. They do not contribute to political parties or political action committees. They do not write letters to congressmen or presidents. They do not register. And finally, they do not vote. They simply refuse to condone the process of majority rule. It is this almost taboo concept that is addressed in the pages of this delightful book.

Many who believe that majority rule is wrong and destructive still argue that it is necessary to vote in self defense. They believe that by voting for candidates that will promise to reduce the size of government, reduce taxes and reduce regulation, the growth of government aggression can be slowed. And, after all, self defense is moral.

Is voting moral if done in self defense?

Substitute "aggression" for "voting" and the question is more properly stated as, "If aggression were an act of self defense, would it be moral?" Well, something can't simultaneously be moral and not moral. The proper question is, "Am I justified in aggressing against B in order to defend myself from aggression by A?" While aggression in the name of self defense is widely accepted, I'm not certain the argument stands up under scrutiny. If a lion is about to attack our group, can others in the group vote to throw me to the lion and claim that it's an act of self defense? If the mugger tells you he's stealing your money to defend himself against his neighbor, or hunger, or illness, does that make his theft morally acceptable?

In spite of the moral arguments, you may still argue that although it might be immoral to vote, if a minor violation of principle could result in a free world, it would be rational to vote. Even though it violates morality, even though political action may be wrong on some ideological level, why don't we just give it a try? What do we have to lose?

Those who are swayed toward political action have forgotten that we have given it a try. It has been tried for thousands of years in thousands of nations, in tens of thousands of elections and

☑ *None of the Above*

through hundreds of thousands of political parties and candidates. Even if political action only had one chance in 100,000 of resulting in a free nation, statistical probability alone would suggest that there would be at least one free nation today. Mankind has reached the brink of self-extinction giving politics a try.

All of political history can be summed up as a struggle to throw the bad guys out and put the good guys in. Just as Sisyphus was condemned to spend eternity in Hades rolling a rock up a hill only to have it roll down again, so the human race seems to be sentenced to spend forever trying to put the good guys in office only to find they turn bad once there. I'm sorry to say, but when it comes to placing power in the hands of humans, there are no good guys. Thus, the most obvious, and therefore most overlooked reason to eschew political action is that it simply doesn't work.

When you talk to the average person about the advantages of a stateless society, the quick retort is that such an idea is utopian; it would never work. Government is required to control man's selfish nature.

Clearly, the truth is precisely the opposite.

Because of the selfish nature of man, it is utopian to give a human being authority over the lives and property of strangers and to expect that person not to consider his or her own well-being

☑ *None of the Above*

first. Because man is genetically programmed to be self-interested, when one man is placed in a position of authority over another, his natural, genetic impulse is to use that authority to his own advantage. Truly, it is utopian to imagine that a government composed of a small number of individuals would consider the well-being of the general population before considering its own. Behind every law passed by politicians, some politician or political supporter benefited. Lord Acton's famous maxim, "Power tends to corrupt and absolute power corrupts absolutely," perfectly describes the history of government. It does so because it is an astute observation about the nature of man.

If you reject the pragmatic arguments, the moral arguments and the scientific evidence that indicates political action must fail because of the nature of man, there is still a compelling and overriding reason to abandon political action.

On a practical and immediate level, political action is always destructive. I once published "Pugsley's First Law of Government." It was: "All government programs accomplish the opposite of what they are designed to achieve." It is a logical corollary that the same is true of political action.

Consistently down through history, all efforts to put the "good guy" in power have resulted in more government, not less — even when the person elected was expressly elected to reduce the size of government. Let us not forget the mood in the United States when Ronald Reagan first ran for president. Here was a popular hero, a man of the people, who rode into Washington on a white horse. His campaign was simple and directly to the point: government was too big, it was taxing too much, it was spending too much, it was strangling the economy with regulations, and it was no longer a servant of the people. His mandate from the American people was clear: balance the federal budget and reduce the size of the federal government.

What was the result?

In 1980 federal spending totaled $613 billion. In 1988, at the end of Ronald Reagan's tenure, it totaled $1,109 billion. In 1980 federal tax revenue was $553 billion. In 1988 it was $972 billion. Total government debt went from $877 billion to $2,661 billion. Then, to prove the ultimate futility of electing a white knight, the electorate decided that the government wasn't doing enough so it put a liberal democrat back in office. All of the rhetoric of the Reagan campaign is forgotten. All of the public anger over the bureaucracy is forgotten. Government is bigger than ever.

The freedom seeker's involvement in politics always will achieve the opposite of the result intended. No matter who the candidate is or what

☑ *None of the Above*

issues motivate him, political action will not reduce state power; it will enhance state power.

Support of political action strengthens the institution of voting. It plays right into the hands of the constituencies that feed on state power — businesses that gain market share through regulations, laws and subsidies; trade unions that depend for survival on coercive labor laws; entitlement recipients who demand their subsidies; welfare recipients; government employees — all are absolutely dependent on the survival of <u>the myth that "you must get out and vote."</u> In the end there will always be more votes for subsidy than voters who will vote to avoid taxes. There will always be more people struggling to get up to the feeding trough than there will be people determined to keep them away. That is simply human nature.

History does not support the hypothesis that electoral politics might lead to a freer society. There is no case of which I am aware where electoral politics has reduced the size and scope of government in a fundamental or lasting sense. <u>Fundamental reductions seem to have come only on the heels of trauma.</u> Wars, depressions or the outright failure of the state have, on occasions, led to dramatic contractions of state power, the recent collapse of the Soviet Union being an example. But none of these failure-induced contractions can be traced to electoral politics.

☑ *None of the Above*

The closest thing to victory that history provides as evidence that political action can be used to control the expansion of the state are the tiny and short-lived slowing of government growth such as happened under Margaret Thatcher in England or in recent years under Finance Minister Roger Douglas in New Zealand. But inevitably, the relief is brief and has never resulted in a continuing erosion of state power. Electoral politics has never succeeded in achieving a free society. So, to all of the other arguments against political action, you can add the evidence of history.

In the end, no matter how forceful, how principled or how scientific the arguments presented, you may say, "Principle and reason be hanged, we have to do something!" You may argue that we can't just stand helplessly by and let the politicians have their way with us. Even if it is immoral, even if it is contrary to man's nature, even if in the long run it is counterproductive, and even if there is no evidence that political action has ever been productive, we have to do something. After all, as one pundit once said, "The only thing necessary for the triumph of evil is for good men to do nothing."

This idea, that something must be done, is a disaster. History is replete with instances in which well-meaning people, intent on doing something, turned their discomfort into catastrophe. In past

☑ *None of the Above*

centuries, doctors, ignorant of causes of many ailments but wanting to do something for their patients, commonly bled them, making a sick patient even sicker. Obstetricians in the mid-nineteenth century, not understanding the cause of "puerperal fever" but eager to do something to stop the fatal disease, gave unsanitary pelvic examinations that spread death from patient to patient. When the Black Plague swept Europe in the fourteenth century, people didn't understand the cause, but in their desire to "do something" they killed the cats and burned the witches.

However, the first rule of medicine is, as Hippocrates said, "at least do no harm." <u>Unless you know that the action you are undertaking is right, you're much better off doing absolutely nothing.</u>

Political action is built on exactly the same false premise as that of a centrally-planned economy: i.e., that an organized group of political activists engaged in a planned group effort can build freedom more rapidly or better than the individual efforts of independently acting people adhering to the principles of free-market economics as outlined in the works of such giants as Adam Smith and Ludwig von Mises. The central theme in their economic philosophy is that the "invisible hand" of the marketplace — the individual efforts of independently acting people — creates progress and plenty; that any attempt to "organize" and

☑ *None of the Above*

"centrally-plan" economic activity subverts progress and eventually leads to tyranny.

If all the energies now being expended on political action by freedom advocates around the world were focused instead on finding individual solutions, on allowing the "invisible hand" free reign, we would marvel at the ideas and mechanisms that would be bound to evolve.

In this delightful, entertaining and amusing book, Sy Leon leads you through the absurdities of the political system. Reading it should make even the most ardent political activist see that the Emporer really isn't wearing any clothes. And along the way, he will show you that you do have alternatives when you are handed a ballot, the first of which is to simply say, "None of The Above."

☑ *None of the Above*

Chapter 1

"The Vanishing Voter: A Look at Non-Voting as a Purposive Act"

by V. Lance Tarrance*

It has been observed that non-voting (and political alienation from government) is a very widespread phenomenon today in the American political culture. There are those today who consider this a serious malfunction of our political system — the argument that if men are to control their destinies they must not only be politically conscious but must also take a hand via the franchise in determining public policy. On the other hand, there are some political theorists who have found "a certain amount" of non-voting and apathy a favorable sign — the argument that this level of non-voting signified a society fundamentally contented and basically stable. Why has concern about non-voting so escalated the traditional de-

---

* Excerpt from a Study by the Institute of Politics, John Fitzgerald Kennedy School of Management, Harvard University. V. Lance Tarrance is former Director of Research for Republican National Committee, and former official of U.S. Census Bureau.

bate, formerly somewhat rarified, into a political practitioner's debate?

The answer is that non-voting is now viewed as a political force which has the potential to alter the entire political system, or at least cause significant modifications in it.

As the degree of both perceived importance of voting (sense of citizen duty) and campaign interest has increased, voting participation has declined. However, it can be assumed that the psychological model did not anticipate the relatively large ticket-splitting phenomenon in recent decades, and the parallel diminution of partisan intensity. It would seem that one must reject the almost axiomatic notion of the past that the rate of turnout increases with political involvement and information consumption.

Most studies of the importance of legal factors in voter turnout have dealt with registration requirements, literacy tests, absentee ballots and the like. The classic work here is by the President's Commission on Registration and Voting (1963) which concluded that the major reason for non-voting was restrictive legislation. The Commission's report, based upon the conventional political wisdom of the day, assumed that restrictive legal and administrative procedures "which disfranchised millions" could be alleviated by a series of legislative and/or judicial steps, a sort of af-

☑ *None of the Above*

firmative action plan, and that, *ipso facto*, would lead to increased turnout. However, decades later, after almost every serious legal prescription has been met, non-voting has increased. We can draw the conclusion that the Commission may have been correct in its humanitarian intentions, but incorrect in its original research hypotheses.

Previous studies that emphasized the importance of interparty competition and electoral competitiveness for voter turnout are largely irrelevant today. This is largely due to their reliance on the Rational Economic Man Theory.

The classic statement of the Rational Economic Man Theory is Anthony Downs' *The Economic Theory of Democracy* (1957). Downs argues that an individual's "long-range participation value" (utility) is a rational basis upon which to vote.

It may be that non-voters are indeed acting "rationally" and that there is no longer a perception of a long-range benefit to voting. For many individuals, the cost of obtaining information to make political decisions may be too high (or inflationary) and the benefits too low (or the money supply too tight). Moreover, as the political-economic arena has become so crowded and confused, it may be that a "long-range participation value" of .00000000001 is not enough to make one feel efficacious today. Downs concludes that abstention from voting is rational only if a citizen believes either *a)* that any policy change in government will have no net effect on his utility income, or *b)* that policy changes may affect his income but there is nothing he feels he can do about it.

One of the least circulated but most relevant studies is one conducted by Morris Rosenberg ("Some Determinants of Political Apathy," *Public Opinion Quarterly*, 1955). Rosenberg found that one factor contributing to political apathy was the feeling that activity is futile — the individual feels that even if he were active, the desired political results would probably not come to pass. Thus, there is no point in doing anything.

Furthermore, as the size of the group increases (e.g., 185 million eligible voters in the United States in 1992), each individual alone makes less of a difference to the totality, and his vote would have little effect on the outcome of the election. And, parallel to this, an individual today senses an "unmanageability" of the political forces — "the government" ignores the will of the people and makes its own decisions almost completely uninfluenced by the people.

Other determinants were identified as the periodicity of American elections which is not resonant with human reactions and emotions, the feeling of a discontinuous sense of control over the political process, and a gap between the ideal and the real (e.g., honesty in government). Rosenberg concludes by saying that the "mass nature of the society, characterized by wide disparities of power, promotes the sense of personal insignificance; the centralization of government fosters a sense of remoteness from the key decision-making processes (some people do not participate actively because of the incertitude of their political convictions; to them politics may be confused, complicated and contradictory, and political communications may be rejected as propaganda)."

Non-voting, when expressed as the "party of the non-voter," has always "won" American elections in this half century (see Tables 1 and 2). There has been an increase of 21 million new non-participants in the two decades ending 1992. Additionally, the election cycle just completed (1992) indicates an average non-voter population of 83 million citizens.*

The upshot of all these new non-voting statistics seems to presage more non-voting.* More non-voting most likely will cause more electoral instability as the political arena is left disproportionately to the partisans with their above-average ideological motivations and polarization of policy preferences. More partisan cleavages generally

---

* Emphasis added.

☑ *None of the Above*

produce more diametrically opposed party nominees which in turn tends to create more political upheavals in the system. These "shock waves" could possibly intersect with the new fault lines of economic frustration and lack of confidence in political institutions to make future election years detonators for further political realignment. Voting participation would, of course, have to increase massively for realignment to actually take place. But the fact that large-scale non-voting is a precondition for realignment is of critical importance to practitioners in future elections.

Non-voting must be certified as a precondition to a larger, perhaps inevitable, change in the political system itself.*

---

* Emphasis added.

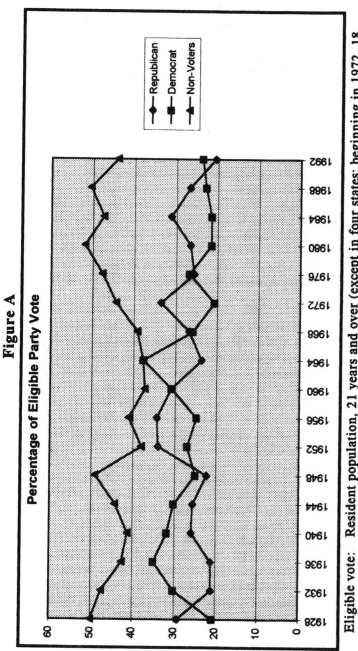

Figure A

Eligible vote: Resident population, 21 years and over (except in four states; beginning in 1972, 18 years and over for all states). Party vote is major party candidate vote.

19

Table 1

The Vanishing Voter: The Presidential Participation Record of Six Decades (Numbered in Millions)

Year	Est. of Eligible Voters	Democratic Party Turnout	Republican Party Turnout	Non-Major Party Turnout	Non-Voter Party	Party of The Winner
1928	72	15	21	—	36	Non-Voter
1932	76	23	16	1	36	Non-Voter
1936	80	28	17	1	34	Non-Voter
1940	85	27	22	—	35	Non-Voter
1944	86	26	22	—	38	Non-Voter
1948	96	24	22	3	47	Non-Voter
1952	100	27	34	—	38	Non-Voter
1956	105	26	36	—	43	Non-Voter
1960	110	34	34	—	41	Non-Voter
1964	114	43	27	—	43	Non-Voter
1968	120	31	32	10	47	Non-Voter
1972	140	29	47	1	62	Non-Voter
1976	146	40	39	—	67	Non-Voter
1980	157	35	43	5	74	Non-Voter
1984	170	37	54	—	79	Non-Voter
1988	178	41	48	—	89	Non-Voter
1992	185	44	39	19	83	Non-Voter

Source: Statistical Abstract of the United States

Table 2
The Vanishing Voter: Percent of the Total Voting Age Population by Party

Year	Democratic Party (%)	Republican Party (%)	Independent (%)	Non-Voter Party (%)
1928	20.8	29.2	—	50.0
1932	30.2	21.1	—	47.4
1936	35.0	21.2	—	42.5
1940	31.8	25.9	—	41.2
1944	30.2	25.6	—	44.2
1948	25.0	22.3	3.0	49.0
1952	27.0	34.0	—	38.0
1956	24.8	34.3	—	41.0
1960	30.9	30.9	—	37.3
1964	37.7	23.7	—	37.7
1968	25.8	26.7	8.0	31.2
1972	20.7	33.6	—	44.3
1976	26.8	25.6	3.0	44.6
1980	21.5	26.6	—	51.9
1984	21.5	31.2	—	47.3
1988	22.8	26.7	—	50.5
1992	23.7	20.6	10.0	44.0

Source: Statistical Abstract of the United States, major candidate vote.

Table 3

The Rise of the Reported Registered Non-Voter[1] (Numbered in Millions)

Election Year	Total Registered	Total Voters	Registered Non-Voters[2]
1976	96	81	15
1980	103	86	17
1984	115	92	23
1988	114	91	23
1992	126	104	21

[1] Because of the over-reporting problem in post-election surveys of voter participation, it can be assumed that the "reported registered non-voter" is understated by several percentage points.

[2] The registered non-voter is important politically as he is assumed to be the precursor of systemic alienation and a "leading indicator" of population participation growth or no-growth. Figures cited are from Current Population Reports, U.S. Census.

☑ *None of the Above*

Chapter 2

None of the Above Is Acceptable

> *"He is free who knows how to keep in his own hands the power to decide, at each step, the course to his life, and who lives in a society which does not block the exercise of that power."*
>
> — Salvador de Madriaga

When is a choice not a choice? When you cannot say "No."

If a thief approaches you on a dark street and says, "Your money or your life," you have alternatives open to you. You can forfeit either your money or your life. But no one is foolish enough to say this represents a real choice. The thief is forcing his idea of choice on you. No matter what you choose, you lose. Unless you can say to the thief, "I don't wish to give you my money or my life" — unless you can choose not to deal with the thief *at all* — you don't have a legitimate choice.

This is pretty obvious — or at least it should be. But the mechanism of common sense often breaks down when we move into the labyrinth of politics, where all passages lead to the same place: the defrauding of the voter.

☑ *None of the Above*

For instance, it is commonly said that the virtue of democracy lies in its providing the voters with a choice as to who represents them in government. But when you go to the ballot box to make your choice, what do you see? You see a list of candidates from which you are supposed to select your favorite. But what if you don't have a favorite? What if you don't want *any* of the candidates to represent you? Can you say "No" to all of the candidates? With the present ballot, that is impossible. But then you don't have a real choice. Where the difference between candidates is less than the difference between Tweedledum and Tweedledee, your supposed choice is as significant as the choice between arsenic and rat poison.

Until a voter can express his disapproval and rejection of all candidates by saying "No" to all of them, the voting apparatus is merely an illusion of a free choice system. Free people have a right to say "No."

To vote at all in the present unrepresentative system does more harm than good. Victorious candidates invariably claim a mandate of the people when no such mandate exists. If a winner receives 70 percent of the vote he will claim a smashing victory over his opponent, and he will claim this shows his enormous support among the populace. Yet only a fraction of the people may have voted in the first place, which means that the

☑ *None of the Above*

winning candidate's percentage represents only a small fraction of the total population. If, for example, over 30 percent of the people vote in an election, the winner's "overwhelming" 70 percent represents only 21 percent of the total populace. So much for his "mandate."

People who have a sincere wish to participate in the voting process seek an opportunity for free and open expression. If the option, "None of the Above is acceptable," were made available on the ballot, it would not interfere with someone actually being elected to office. Under our present plurality system, it is not necessary to gain a *fixed number* of votes to win; a candidate wins by getting more votes than his opponent(s). Thus it is conceivable (in an extreme situation) that 90 percent of the voters might vote "No," and of the remaining 10 percent, 6 percent vote for candidate "A" and 4 percent for candidate "B." Candidate "A" would then be elected to office.

But consider the powerful effect on the new office holder who must face the publicized fact that 94 percent of those who voted said, in effect, "We don't want you and we don't approve of your policies." The result would be that the newly elected official would spend less time crowing about his popularity and more time trying to find out what the people want. Massive public disapproval is probably the ultimate weapon available

☑ *None of the Above*

to us in our defense against oppressive and offensive political power seekers.

Additionally, the ballot amendment would be more effective than the write-in method because the "No" voters would be counted and visible (as write-ins are not) and would be part of the publicized election returns.

At present, a vast number of people find they can only vote for the least distasteful candidate. This negative vote is the *conscious* choice of the lesser of two evils. The consequence of making an evil choice is that we wind up with evil. Meanwhile, those who refuse to vote for the lesser evil, those who abstain from voting altogether, find themselves disenfranchised. In this alleged democracy, the disenfranchised majority finds itself without a voice. This is the real silent majority.

The winning candidate, of course, invariably alludes to this silent majority as approving of him, but his claim would be impossible if the silent majority had the opportunity to remain silent no longer, and to voice their opposition at the polls by voting "No." Faced with a preponderance of votes against him, the politician, stripped of his illusory mandate, would be forced to assume more personal responsibility for his actions and to account for his actions to his constituents.

Why would anyone oppose the "None of the Above is Acceptable" option? — except the poli-

☑ *None of the Above*

ticians who are afraid of what the silent majority will say, given the opportunity. Which brings us to a major issue. Are the silent majority silent because they have nothing to say, or because they have no means to express their dissatisfaction? Ungag the silent majority, let them express their own opinions instead of having the "choices" of political parties shoved down their throats, let them say "No" to all of the candidates and this question will be settled once and for all.

We must never lose sight of the basic issue here. Choice is subjective; it occurs in the mind of the individual. When a political gang meets in a back room and draws up a list of candidates, that list represents the gang's choice, not ours. The "choice" given by the politicians to the voters is a farce; it is a variation of "Heads I win, tails you lose." Unless we can voice our own opinions at the ballot box instead of being chained by a politician's idea of what a choice is, we are political dupes, not free individuals.

But might not the "None of the Above" option harm the two-party system in America? Perhaps, but the right to vote exists to give the people a choice, not to protect the two-party system. Free choice is the basic issue here, not the self-serving concerns of two power-laden political parties. The "None of the Above" option is not only consistent

☑ *None of the Above*

with the right to vote — it is an indispensable part of it.

But isn't the "None of the Above" option a negative idea, destructive to America? Far from it. If politicians are really as concerned as they say they are with representing people, how can they do this if they don't know what the people think? The "None of the Above" option simply opens the lines of communication; it permits citizens to express dissatisfaction with their purported representatives — and who can honestly oppose this, unless politicians don't give a damn about what the people think? Politicians can't have it both ways: If they really care about their constituents, they must favor every opportunity to facilitate better communication. This is the central purpose of the "None of the Above" option. If, on the other hand, politicians couldn't care less about their constituents, then they won't champion the "None of the Above" option. But then let's have no more of their deceitful and idiotic rhetoric about being dedicated "public servants."

But in the final analysis, it may be asked, will the "None of the Above" option do any good? Won't politicians ignore it after they are in office, as they seem to ignore everything else? Yes, this is a real possibility. We can try to control politicians but we can't change their nature. At the very least, however, we would know *what* is being ig-

☑ *None of the Above*

nored. It would be unmistakably obvious to everyone that the elected official lacks moral scruples. Few people would take him seriously after that point, and his chances for re-election would be severely damaged.

A choice between the politicians is not a choice — it is a surrender. Until there is a legitimate choice, there should be no vote. Until such time as the political process is truly representative, until such time as the ballots are amended to include the option, "None of the Above is Acceptable," there should be a massive voters' boycott. This applies to all primary, county, state and national elections.

So let's insist on our right of free speech in the electoral process; let's insist on the right to vote "No" in every election. The politicians may not like what we have to say, but so what? We are not here to please them — they are supposed to please us. Ungag the voters, and the politicians will see just how "pleased" we are.

☑ *None of the Above*

Chapter 3

The Lesser of Two Evils

If you were to ask the average person on the street, "What is the first thing that comes to your mind when I say 'the lesser of two evils'?" he would probably answer, "Politics!" After decades of watching the sideshow of political campaigning, millions of Americans no longer believe the politicians when they dust off their promises and flash their toothy grins for the election year charades. In voting booths all over the country, people are sighing in resignation and voting for a candidate who is the lesser of two (or three or four) evils. Understandably, the voter feels frustrated. He wants to have a say in who governs him, but the only choices available are the handpicked henchmen of the political parties.

Politicians are aware of the widespread voter disenchantment; they are aware of the small turnouts at the polls and they do not like it. For politicians need participation — they need to create the illusion of majority support so they can continue the myth of being the "people's choice." It is not surprising, then, that the politicians band

☑ *None of the Above*

together and urge everyone to vote, even if it means voting for someone you don't really want. We are encouraged to believe that we are violating a sacred duty if we do not vote. We are encouraged, in effect, to choose the lesser of two evils.

What does it mean to say "the lesser of two evils"? Basically, it means that you are faced with an alternative where no matter how you choose, you end up with something that is, by your own standards, evil. For a choice to be the lesser of two evils, you must personally evaluate both alternatives as evil, but choose one of them anyway.

Choosing the lesser of two evils may, in extremely unusual circumstances, be necessary. If you are stranded in the wilderness with your two pet dogs, you may have to decide to eat one of the dogs in order to remain alive. To select either would obviously be a repulsive choice, although it might be your only chance of staying alive. But if there were a third option, such as hunting down a wild rabbit, you would obviously choose this without question. To select the lesser of two evils when there is a third option available to you that is not evil, is a destructive and self-defeating course of action.

Unfortunately, many people take precisely this destructive course of action when it comes to voting. A person may judge, by his personal stan-

☑ *None of the Above*

dards, both candidates for political office to be evil, and he may resign himself to voting for the lesser of two evils. But the lesser of two evils in this case is still evil, *by the voter's own standards*. If a voter endorses an evil candidate, he gives him his sanction and support; he encourages the politician, as his representative, to promote evil in his name. As more and more people come to realize this, and as more and more people refuse to be intimidated into sanctioning a politician they dislike and disapprove of, a greater number of people are boycotting the voting process out of frustration and disgust. This trend is likely to continue until we are provided with a true option at the polls — until we can vote *"None of the Above is Acceptable."*

Until a legitimate choice is offered at the polls, until we can express our disapproval of all the candidates running for office, to vote in an election where you disapprove of all the candidates can have no other consequence than to foster and promote actions of which you disapprove. We are not in an emergency situation; we are not forced to vote for one candidate or another. There is another choice available to us at present, and that is not to vote at all. Under the current system, this is the only reasonable alternative when you disapprove of political candidates. Non-voting as a conscious, deliberate choice is the only rational

☑ *None of the Above*

and constructive way in which we can exercise our freedom of choice, as long as the ballot does not provide true freedom of choice. This, then, is the alternative to voting for the lesser of two evils: not to vote at all.

Voting is meant to be a positive, not a negative process. It is supposed to be a way for the citizens of this country to have a say in their government. But the politicians have subverted the purpose of the voting process. By giving only the *illusion* of a real choice at the polls, they have forced those who want to vote to select the least among evils.

Another disturbing aspect of this is that people's expectations have been lowered to the point where they no longer expect to find men and women of stature on the ballot. We are no longer surprised to find that a candidate is more charlatan than sage. Our expectations have been beaten down after years of scandal and disappointment. It is not surprising to see the politicians' stature shrinking in direct proportion to our lowered expectations. And these things combine into a prescription ensuring that elections will produce more and more evil.

Elections, however, were not intended to encourage evil, and they need not continue to do so. But if we are going to vote, we must have a genuine choice. Then, and only then, can we begin

☑ *None of the Above*

to purge some of the evil from the electoral process. A good place to start, as we have said earlier in this chapter, is to insist that "None of the Above" be placed on all ballots. Then those who disapprove of all the candidates can still participate in the electoral process without having to choose among degrees of evil.

In addition, the "None of the Above" option will permit us to express disapproval of dishonest politicians. This might promote better behavior and eventually lead to a better quality of candidates. And, most important, the "None of the Above" option will permit voting to reflect what the general public really wants (or, in most cases, *doesn't* want) instead of indicating, as it now does, only the desires of a small percentage of voters who are permitted to choose among candidates groomed by a massive, impersonal and unresponsive political machine.

☑ *None of the Above*

Chapter 4

Politicalese — The Language of Deceit

"Do we not continually hear them quote Blackstone's assertion that 'no subject of England can be constrained to pay any aids or taxes even for the defense of the realm or the support of government, but such as are imposed by his own consent, or that of his representative in parliament'? And what does this mean? It means, say they, that every man should have a vote. True, but it means much more. If there is any sense in words it is a distinct enunciation of the very right now contended for. In affirming that a man may not be taxed unless he has directly or indirectly given his consent, it affirms that he may refuse to be so taxed; and to refuse to be taxed is to cut all connection with the state. Perhaps it will be said that this consent is not a specific, but a general one, and that the citizen is understood to have assented to everything his representative may do when he voted for him. But suppose he did not vote for him, and on the contrary did all in his power to get elected someone holding opposite views — what then? The reply will probably be that, by taking part in such an election, he tacitly agreed to abide by the decision of the majority. And how if he did not vote at all? Why then he cannot justly complain of any tax, seeing that he made no protest against its imposition. So, curiously enough, it seems that he gave his consent in whatever way he acted — whether he said yes,

☑ None of the Above

whether he said no, or whether he remained neuter! A rather awkward doctrine, this. Here stands an unfortunate citizen who is asked if he will pay money for a certain proffered advantage; and whether he employs the only means of expressing his refusal or does not employ it, we are told that he practically agrees, if only the number of others who agree is greater than the number of those who dissent. And thus we are introduced to the novel principle that A's consent to a thing is not determined by what A says, but by what B may happen to say!"
— Herbert Spencer
Social Statics
1878, Chapter 19

Perhaps the greatest achievement of the human race was the invention of language. As a result of man's desire to communicate and cooperate with his fellow humans, there have evolved thousands of different languages and dialects. These two goals — communication and cooperation — usually go hand in hand. But language is used to communicate accurately only if one desires willing cooperation. Unfortunately, some people would rather manipulate and control others than acquire their voluntary cooperation. They will employ language for the purpose of deceit, and use words to obscure and distort, not to explain and clarify. It is not surprising, therefore, that those who engage in deceit and dishonesty as a way of life — politicians — have invented a language of their own to serve their goals. I call this language

☑ None of the Above

"Politicalese" — the language of politics, the language of deceit.

It is obvious, from what has been said previously, that politicians are not interested in cooperating with people. Politicians prefer to impose their life styles on others; they seek to control and manipulate. Quite naturally, therefore, politicians will adopt a language tailored for deceit.

A good illustration of Politicalese is found in the movie "Robin Hood." In the opening scene, Robin Hood crashes a banquet given by the evil Sheriff of Nottingham for the politicians and bureaucrats of that day. Robin Hood, in the best tradition of swashbucklers, denounces the lot as a band of looters and thieves. "You speak treason!" shouts one of the crowd, to which Robin Hood replies with a magnificent line, "Yes, fluently."

Robin Hood was accused with one of the favorite words in the arsenal of Politicalese — "treason." What did his treason consist of? It consisted of calling something what it is. Taxation, as Robin Hood saw, was really theft, and this made the politicians who imposed and collected taxes, thieves.

Such clear-headed thinking was dangerous to politicians then, and it is dangerous to them now. Politicians have a vested interest in vague, sloppy language; they use it themselves and they encourage its use by others. In this way they hope to

☑ *None of the Above*

cloak their criminal activities in the mystique of law and governmental legitimacy.

What are some of the terms of Politicalese? "Apathy," a term discussed elsewhere in this book at length, is among the favorites. Non-voters are said to be apathetic, when in fact they are simply fed up with the illusion of choice at the ballot box, where no choice exists. But to state the truth in plain language, to say honestly that many people do not vote because they don't like the alternatives presented, is too dangerous for the politicians, so they condemn non-voters as "apathetic."

The "public good" and the "public welfare" — these and similar phrases are among the most common of Politicalese jargon. Has there ever been a politician who has not claimed that his actions, regardless of how self-serving, were really for the "public good"? Such phrases have no real meaning; or, to put it another way, they can mean anything you want them to. Their function is to justify and whitewash even the most nefarious political deeds.

"Mandate of the people" — this bit of Politicalese means that one politician got more votes than another. The total number of votes he received may actually have represented less than five percent of those eligible to vote — but no matter. He claims a "mandate of the people" nonetheless. He represents, by his own decree, the

☑ *None of the Above*

entire population. His enemies and opponents, comprising a large segment of the public, are now transformed into his "constituency." Such is the magical translating power of Politicalese.

The "draft" — this, of course is an age-old favorite. To "draft" someone is to force them into military life against their will. It is involuntary servitude; in other words, kidnapping and slavery.

"Public duty" and "the national interest" — these are Politicalese terms to justify other Politicalese terms, such as the draft and taxation. "National security" is a similar phrase, commonly used to obfuscate intrusions and violations of our homes and our privacy, such as wiretapping and burglary.

"Conspiracy" — that means to talk with others about defending yourself against politicians.

"Assassination" — that means to kill a politician. If you kill an ordinary person, even a very important person, it is murder. But to kill a politician presumably is worse, so it requires a special, odious term. "War" is what we have when politicians and generals decide to kill others on a massive scale. In war, of course, it is all right to kill. The politicians have voted on it and given it their approval, so morality is suspended temporarily. Even the basic standards of human decency are forced into suspended animation through the verbal legerdemain of Politicalese.

☑ *None of the Above*

"Domestic policy" — that is Politicalese for a politician meddling in the affairs of his won countrymen. "Foreign policy" is when a politician meddles in the affairs of another country.

"Public service" — is any business which has been granted a monopoly by the government, and which is therefore expensive and inefficient. Such an organization doesn't render good service or satisfactory service, as regular businesses must do in order to survive. The post office, for instance, is said to render a "public service." In other words, it is wasteful and a drain on the taxpayers, but the politician wants to keep it immune from competition nonetheless. Why? So he can render a personal service to his political friends by giving them juicy appointments running these "public services." By padding the public payroll with his friends, the politician has created more "public servants" — and we, of course, are expected to be enthusiastically grateful.

"Eminent domain" — that is when your property is stolen by politicians for the "public good." And who decides what constitutes the "public good?" The politicians, naturally.

"Legal tender" — that is what the government calls its paper certificates. How do we know the certificates are good? We have the politicians' word on it! Now doesn't that make you feel secure? "Counterfeiter" — that is the label given to

None of the Above

one who competes with government in the cranking out of worthless scraps of paper. Since the government presumably hires better artists, it is often able to distinguish "legal tender" from "counterfeit money." This superior artwork, along with the mystical blessing given to "legal tender" by the politicians, is the only thing that distinguishes it from "counterfeit money."

This is only a sampling of Politicalese; you can undoubtedly think of many more examples. What can we do about it? Not much — the politicians will continue to use it whether we like it or not. But at least we can learn the art of translating Politicalese into honest language. In fact, we might even insist that all politicians travel with a translator during election campaigns. The politician could deliver a line of his speech and pause while the translator makes it intelligible. Or, if this is too inconvenient, perhaps the listeners could be provided with earphones through which a translator speaks at the same time as the politician. Whatever method is adopted, however, it is bound to be an improvement.

Chapter 5

"The Good Of Society"

"It is for the good of society" — how many times have we heard this phrase as a political justification for curtailing our freedom and taking our money? If a politician said he was going to take our money to feed his brother-in-law or to buy himself a new yacht, we would protest. But all a politician has to do is preface his remarks with "for the good of society," and somehow even the most untenable schemes become plausible. But what is "society"? Does it make sense to justify anything in the name of "society"?

A society is a group of individuals viewed collectively, or abstractly. Without individuals there is no society, and society is nothing over and above these individuals. A society is not a distinct entity like a human being, and to speak of the good of society is to speak metaphorically. What we really mean is that something is good for the individuals within that society. If freedom of choice is good for individuals, then it is good for society. All it means to say that something is good

☑ *None of the Above*

or bad for society is that something is good or bad for individuals.

When looking at social issues, a guiding principle to keep in mind is that if an action is not proper for an individual, then it is not proper for that action to be taken in the name of society. If it is not proper for you to tell your neighbor how to run his life, then it is not proper for "society" to do this either. Politically, "the good of society" is used as a cover-up for taking actions that the public would not tolerate under other circumstances. Politicians want us to believe that, when considering "the good of society," ordinary standards of behavior and evaluation don't apply. But "society" is just a way of describing a group of individuals, and the "the good of society" is a metaphor, not a reality.

It is always the individual who feels the effect of political action. When a politician talks about certain measures benefiting society, all he is saying is that his measures will benefit certain people. But whenever there is a beneficiary of political action, there is also a victim who is left to pick up the tab. When we see that political action for the good of society consists of taking from some people for the benefit of others, the altruistic language of politicians seems much less impressive.

☑ *None of the Above*

But isn't it true that there are problems of society that must be dealt with by politicians? No. Social problems are nothing more than individual problems magnified a million times; and when exaggerated to this degree it appears that we need an army of politicians and bureaucrats to deal with them. In fact, however, even these problems are best dealt with on an individual basis. Imagine, for instance, what would happen if the mayor of New York City decided that selecting what to eat for breakfast every day was a "social problem" and that it was the duty of government to solve it. Think of the size of the agency required to oversee the selection of food for millions of New Yorkers every morning, and think of the tremendous expense and waste involved. In addition, there would be many dissatisfied people who either would not get what they wanted or would not get any breakfast at all.

In the present situation, by leaving what is an individual problem to individual choice, millions of New Yorkers decide what to eat for breakfast, and how to provide and obtain it, perfectly well without the unwanted intervention of politicians. All problems, in the final analysis, are like this. Society has no problems, only individuals do. To arbitrarily multiply individual problems, and then lump those problems together as a "social issue," is to open the door for disaster. It makes issues

☑ *None of the Above*

seem so overwhelming and complicated that the politician is taken seriously each time he calls for more bureaucratic meddling.

Remember that whether or not something is a problem for you depends on your subjective estimation. Selecting what to eat for breakfast is not a problem for you if you choose not to eat breakfast. The fact that there is not a park in a given area of the city is not a problem for you, if you do not regard it as a problem. Thus, whenever a politician defines something as a problem facing society, thereby implying that it is a problem for you as an individual, he is abrogating your right to pass your own judgment, and to decide for yourself what is or is not a "problem."

The continued employment of politicians depends on their creating more fictitious problems to solve, so it is not surprising that they are constantly pulling new social problems out of the closet. Upon examining these social problems, we find that someone somewhere is dissatisfied about something and they want the government to do something about it. Well, what person does not have unresolved problems? This means that every personal problem is potentially a social issue for the politician, which gives him an inexhaustible supply of issues to blow out of proportion in an effort to keep himself busy.

☑ *None of the Above*

Whenever we are told that society is confronted with immense difficulties, we should listen carefully and dig beneath the surface. We should see if the social problem is actually a number of individual problems magnified to a ridiculous degree. And we should see if we really need this or that new bureaucratic agency to "solve" the problem — an agency that will probably grow to a monstrous size.

Freedom of choice is the area most commonly attacked under the banner of "the good of society." Almost every new political proposal limits our freedom of choice in one way or another. We are told that some of our freedom must be sacrificed for the good of society. But if freedom of choice is good for the individual, which it is, then it must be good for society; for as we have seen, these two things cannot be separated. Likewise, if restricting freedom is harmful to the individual, which it is, then it must be bad for society. There is no way out of this conclusion. Nothing can be good for society if it is not good for the individual.

In this age of specialization, politicians would have us believe that there are specialists in social problems and that we should turn to them for expert guidance. But when we realize that social problems break down into problems of individuals, and when we realize that no one knows better than

☑ *None of the Above*

you how to deal with your own life, we see clearly that the politician's alleged expertise is a farce. He may try to dazzle you with impressive committee investigations, culminating in reams of useless statistics and "expert" testimony. But in the final analysis, you must live your life, and you must be in a position to make the important decisions that affect your life. You do not require reams of statistics and a panel of authorities to tell you how to live.

So the next time more of your freedom is stolen and you are told it is for the good of society, take a closer look at what "society" represents. You will find that whatever the politician means by "society," he does not mean you.

☑ *None of the Above*

Chapter 6

Where The Individual Vote Really Counts

It is fashionable these days to criticize governmental agencies and regulations. Even those who believe in the ability of government to solve our problems take swipes at the incredible bureaucratic waste and mismanagement that occurs whenever a government "business" or regulatory agency decides to set up shop. Some politicians go so far as to support a "sunset" provision whereby agencies would have to justify their existence, say, every four years, or pass into oblivion.

Politicians, here and elsewhere, are taking a stand which they believe to be popular with the voters. We have become increasingly aware that business regulations, such as we find in various industries, which are supposed to "protect" the consumer from sundry evils, actually serve only to protect established firms from competing with other, more efficient or less costly businesses. Thus the consumer ends up paying more, not only for the service in question, but also for the support of the regulatory agencies themselves.

☑ *None of the Above*

The same is true of government "services" in general. Anyone who has stood in line for what seems an eternity at a Department of Motor Vehicles or a post office, knows just how efficient these services are. And anyone who has tangled with an irate bureaucratic clerk, who need not worry about competition, knows just how courteous they can be.

With these everyday annoyances common to everyone, politicians invariably strike a responsive chord whenever they promise, as part of their campaign platforms, to minimize bureaucratic waste and inefficiency. The politicians, we are told, will clean up the bureaucracy if only we will vote for them. It is through the power of the vote, then, that we are supposed to express our wishes in regard to government agencies and services.

This is basically a sound idea. We should be able to make our desires known through a vote. But what the politicians fail to recognize is that we don't need them in order to do this. On the contrary, we cast dozens of votes every day without so much as one politician crossing our path. And this non-political voting system is so direct and efficient that the political method of voting is pale by comparison.

This remarkable voting system is economic, and the ballot is the dollar. Each time we buy something, we cast a vote in support of the company providing that product or service, thereby enabling it to stay in business. If we do not like a product, we do not buy it, thus casting a "no" vote. If we do like the product, we buy it, thus casting a "yes" vote. And if we don't like any brand of a particular item, we don't have to buy anything, thereby abstaining from the vote altogether.

With the economic vote there is no need for "sunset" provisions. A business operating on the principles of a voluntary market will succeed only as long as its customers remain satisfied. A shoe manufacturer need not prove its usefulness to a band of politicians. Its usefulness is reinforced every day, as consumers continue to buy its product. If and when consumers withhold their economic vote, the business will quickly disappear.

If those who support and advocate the political system of voting are as enamored as they claim to be about the sanctity of the vote, and if they want voting to express the will of the people, then consistency demands that they champion the economic vote above the political vote. They should institute steps to accelerate moving governmental services and agencies to the private sector, where consumers can voice their satisfaction or dissatisfaction directly by either supporting or not supporting those agencies. This, of course, would be a dangerous political move because politicians are

☑ *None of the Above*

well aware that the vast majority of government activities could not sustain themselves in a voluntary market. Indeed, this is especially true of the "services" provided by politicians themselves. If subjected to an economic vote, whereby we had a choice of whether to hire a politician or not, politicians would quickly find themselves in the unemployment line.

But, it may be asked, isn't this just crass materialism? Why should everything be reduced to the crude level of dollars and cents? It is, after all, quite possible that many government services are worthwhile even if they could not survive in the private sector.

In response to this, we should note that the economic vote is not just a matter of dollars and cents, any more than the political vote is just a matter of pulling a lever in a voting booth. True, we cast our economic votes through dollars and cents, just as we cast our political votes by pulling levers, but that money is simply the means by which we make our desires known. The economic vote is important because it represents free choice. Each time we make a purchase, by casting an economic vote, we express a preference and make our desires known. This is the means by which we control our own destiny and determine the course of our lives. And, in the final analysis, isn't this what self-rule is supposed to be about?

☑ *None of the Above*

There is an argument in favor of political voting to the effect that although voting for politicians to represent us and make our decisions is not desirable, voting on the issues themselves — in the form of propositions — is a direct way of expressing our choices. It eliminates the political "middlemen" and lets the individual voter choose, for instance, whether or not tax revenue should be used for education, whether or not the use of nuclear energy should be forbidden, and so on. It's a good argument, too, as far as it goes. It just doesn't go far enough. Again, when we vote on the various propositions, we decide the issues not just for ourselves but for others. If the majority of voters are opposed to something, they are making a choice for the rest, who favor it. It is only in the economic marketplace that the *individual* vote really counts.

Most of us are aware of the pitfalls of committee action. The larger the committee, the more confusing and unsatisfactory the results of its decisions. And the largest, most inefficient committee of all is the voting public. History shows that most progress has occurred in spite of public opinion, not because of it.

If the introduction of electricity, supermarkets, airplanes, and an endless list of inventions that improved the quality of life, had been put to a vote, we'd be without them today. Only because

☑ *None of the Above*

an individual got an idea and *was free* to risk his own time and money to implement it, has a wider range of choices been made available to the public. And when the public, on an individual basis, rejected the product offered by an individual, only he had to bear the cost involved.

If the decision to produce Volkswagens and Rolls Royces had been put to a vote, most people would have rejected them: The former would have been too ugly and too cheap for other cars to compete with it; the latter too unnecessarily luxurious. But it wasn't up to the public *en masse*, only as individuals — and as individuals the public "voted" in their favor. The consequence of this individual, *economic* vote is a wider range of choice, an increased number of jobs and a greater wealth circulating in the economy. If the public had cast its economic votes against them (as it did with the Edsel), they would have been removed from the market and only the individual businessmen promoting them would have suffered.

Why is the economic vote superior to the political vote? First, we are able to buy a finished product; we are not voting merely for a promise to do something, which is all we ever get from politicians. When we buy a service, we have a contractual guarantee that the service will be performed satisfactorily, which is something no politician dares to do.

☑ *None of the Above*

Second, we have true choice with our economic vote. We can abstain from voting altogether by refusing to buy any brand of a particular item. No product or service can be forced upon us. If we dislike or disagree with what is being offered, we are not forced to pay for it or use it. This, unfortunately, is the opposite of what occurs in politics.

Third, we vote only for ourselves, not for other people. Through the economic vote we express our personal preferences, but we do not make decisions for other people. They are as free as we are to choose for themselves.

Fourth, we can vote every day, and we can continually revise our vote in the face of new information. If we decide from one day to the next that we do not like a product, or that we like another product better, we can put our decision into effect immediately. This is not the case, however, with the political vote. We can cast our political vote only once every several years, and we are stuck with the decision in the meantime.

Fifth, we can vote for particulars with our economic vote. We can cast one vote for the kind of detergent we want, another vote for the kind of television set we want, and so forth. This allows us to retain complete control over our lives. When we elect a political candidate on the other hand, he presumes to make specific choices for us. We do not have that fine-tuning control with which the economic vote provides us.

Finally, through the economic vote we are able to express our desires directly, without using an intermediary. With the political vote, however, another person claims to act in our behalf, and we are forced to pay for his services through money stolen by taxation.

These are only a few of the advantages of the economic vote. But even if the politician agrees that the economic vote is superior to the political vote in many respects, he may offer the final defense that we need some of each. The economic vote and the political vote, he may argue, should exist side by side.

The problem with this suggestion is that it is impossible. The economic and political vote are not only different, they are incompatible. The key to the economic vote is the voluntary consent and cooperation of all participants. The aim of economic voting is to satisfy all parties concerned through a process of mutual exchange. Herein lies the power of economic voting to satisfy individual desires, and herein lies its basic antagonism to the political process.

As is made clear in other chapters of this book, political voting is a process whereby one group of people attempts to force its desires on the rest of the people in a country. The more areas of our

☑ *None of the Above*

lives that are determined by political voting, the less individual choice we have. This is, after all, the problem with governmental agencies, which are the consequence of political rather than economic voting, with the result that they are totally insensitive to consumer desires and demands. We are prevented from exercising our economic vote with these agencies for the simple reason that free choice has been pushed aside by political decree.

In advocating a voters' boycott we are referring to the political vote. We oppose voting not because we want people to have less say in their own affairs but because we want them to have more say. In other words, the less political voting we have, the more economic voting will be possible. And the more we are able to vote economically, the more choice we have. Opposition to the political vote, therefore, is really a positive program aimed at enriching each of our lives.

None of the Above ☑

Chapter 7

The Political Mystique

> *"Is a young man bound to serve his country in war? In addition to his legal duty there is perhaps also a moral duty, but it is very obscure. What is called his country is only its government, and that government consists merely of professional politicians, a parasitical and anti-social class of men. They never sacrifice themselves for their country. They make all wars but very few of them ever die in one. If it is the duty of a young man to serve his country under all circumstances, then it is equally the duty of an enemy young man to serve his. Thus we come to a moral contradiction and absurdity, so obvious that even clergymen and editorial writers sometimes notice it."*
>
> — H.L. Mencken
> *Minority Report* (Knopf, 1956)
> page 173

Government is enveloped in a foggy mystique. Politicians, bureaucrats, judges — virtually all governmental agents of significant power — are treated with a deference and respect that are unknown in the private sector. A president of the United States is addressed as "Mr. President," whereas the president of a corporation, regardless of its size, is called by his real name. A judge is

None of the Above ☑

addressed as "Your Honor," and disrespect to a judge, as judged by the judge himself, can land you in jail for contempt of court. Even the physical setting of a government meeting adds to the political mystique. A judge, dressed in a somber black robe, is seated at a level higher than the rest of the courtroom, and people must rise to their feet when he enters the room. Similarly, most Senate and House hearings place the politicians on an elevated level, clearly indicating their superior position in relation to the rest of the people involved.

Why does government demand this respect? Perhaps it is because government deals with serious, life-and-death issues. But many professional people who have nothing to do with government deal with life-and-death issues as well. You may trust your life to a surgeon or to an airline pilot, but you are not expected to treat surgeons and airline pilots as if they were minor deities.

The exaggerated respect given to those in positions of governmental power is especially strange when we remember that, in theory at least, we the taxpayers are the employers, while those in government are our employees, or "servants." Yet how many employers address their hired help as "Sir," or "Your Honor," or "Mr. President"? Did you ever try to get an appointment with one of your "employees" in government? Did you ever try to fire one? Since when are "employees" allowed to determine their own salary? Something is amiss here. Isn't it possible that politicians and bureaucrats are not the "public servants" they claim to be? Considering that we must pay homage to them, that we must deal with them at their convenience and on their terms, and that they have the power to slap us in jail if we disobey their wishes, wouldn't it be more accurate to say that we are "political servants"? In other words, we must serve the politicians; we must give them money and obey their commands. To say, under these conditions, that politicians and bureaucrats are our servants, is surely one of the worst frauds ever perpetrated on mankind.

Why is this fraud so widely accepted? This is where the political mystique comes in. Throughout history, politicians of all stripes have attempted to sanctify and legitimize their actions. In the early days of man, one warlike tribe would conquer another and the captives were often slain. It soon became apparent, however, that this was an unproductive use of a vanquished people. Why not enslave them, or exact tribute from them? Why not make the captives work for you?

But to maintain this kind of stranglehold over a population requires a considerable amount of power, and tribal chieftains soon found it more expedient to cloak themselves in legitimacy — to convince the subjugated people that they should do as they were told. Offer yourself as a deity, or as God's right-hand man, and in obeying you the people will simply be following their religion. But this "divine right of kings" eventuality lost its appeal, so the politicians had to search elsewhere for legitimacy. They found it in the idea of democracy. Offer yourself to a vote of the people, create the illusion that you represent the will of the majority, and you have created a powerful new mystique. You claim to embody the will of the people, so anyone who opposes you is an enemy of the people. This is a neat trick, and politicians have been using it to their advantage for many, many years.

But why must politicians resort to such illusions? The head of a giant corporation does not find it necessary to legitimize his activities by saying that he has a mandate from the people. He simply runs his business and offers his goods and services to the public, which is free to accept or reject them. Why, then, must the politician look for a mystical sanction?

The answer is that the politician, unlike the ordinary person who works for a living, forces himself on other people whether they want his "services" or not. The politician uses money taken by force as he sees fit. He claims to be rendering a service to the public, but what kind of service is it

None of the Above ☑

that you are forced to accept? The activities of the politician are impositions, not services.

The basic rule of the private sector is exchange. If you want something from someone else, you must pay a mutually agreed-upon price. This is how we get what we want. But some people don't want to exert the effort required to get the consent of others, so they employ political force instead of trade and mutual agreement. This is the case when "big business" turns to government for legislation to protect itself against competition. The results are tariffs, licenses, controls, restrictions and other forms of coercive interference in free exchange. These regulations, we are told, protect us from "cutthroat competition"; but upon closer examination we see that "cutthroat competition" is defined as when your competitor is doing better than you are. Hence, in the name of consumer protection, many businesses call on the strong arm of government to protect *themselves* against other businesses. In the meantime, consumers bear the brunt of higher prices (a consequence of decreased competition) and higher taxes (to pay for the enforcement of regulation).

It is because the politician imposes his bogus services on people that he finds it necessary to legitimize his actions. People are not willing to pay for his "services" voluntarily, so he will twist some arms. But the people whose arms are being twisted are liable to get angry, especially when the politician reaches for their money as well. So what does the politician do now?

Like the tribal chieftain, the politician finds that to twist a few million arms takes a lot of energy and manpower — more than he can muster — so it is more convenient to resort to brainwashing. He resorts to political mystification. Twist issues and common sense instead of arms. Convince those who oppose you, or who eye you suspiciously, that you represent the will of the people. Your opponents are unpatriotic, treasonous, or ungrateful for the "benefits" you seek to force upon them. You represent the good of society, or the good of the country — any number of ridiculous mystifications will serve the purpose.

And so the hoax continues. The politicians rule while claiming to serve. They extort while claiming to administer funds. They wreak havoc while claiming to protect. They serve and serve and serve, and we suffer and suffer and suffer. Could we throw the bunglers out? Perhaps, but this is useless if they are immediately to be replaced by a new set of bunglers. Until we rid ourselves of the political mystique, until we penetrate the smokescreen generated by the political process, until we identify politicians for what they *are* instead of what they *claim* to be, we will continue to suffer the circus of lies and deception known as politics.

None of the Above ☑

Chapter 8

The World's Oldest Profession

To understand the blight of politicians upon our society, we must examine their training, their background and their psychology. Where do politicians come from? Are they delivered by a malicious stork, or is there some other explanation? Actually, there's a simple answer: The vast majority of politicians start out as lawyers.

Is this mere coincidence? By no means. In pursuing his career, the budding lawyer learns the tricks of the trade: he penetrates the foggy mystique of law. He learns its language, its rituals, and — above all — he learns to make it pay, not merely in terms of money but in terms of the power and psychological satisfaction he derives from authoritarian relationships.

Of course, there are some lawyers who enter and practice law to defend the victims of political power. My remarks are not directed at them, but rather at the majority of men and women who, even if they have no political aspirations, form a special elite to take advantage of the average person by offering services that would be unnecessary

None of the Above ☑

in a sane system. Much of the time, those services are required simply to fend off the artificial devices which the state militates against the citizen. The only possible beneficiary of these devices is the attorney, who comes to the rescue of his "helpless" client.

When the average person confronts a legal problem, he is dumbfounded; the law is hopelessly complex and incomprehensible to him; a twisted maze in which he is bound to get lost without a guide. And behold: here comes the lawyer-guide, a trained specialist who will take our friend in hand and show him the way. "Trust me completely," says the lawyer, "and I'll look out for your interests." Is the client right or wrong? Is what he seeks just or unjust? Banish these thoughts from your mind. The lawyer cannot be concerned with such things. He's concerned not with justice but with winning his case by whatever means possible. This is what he is paid for, after all. And should his client lose — well then, his client pays all the more.

In the legal mind, the law is an elaborate chess game with the clients as pawns. The "major pieces" are the various judge-bishops and attorney-knights who move the pawns about in the castle-courthouses at their bidding. Being an expert in the game makes the lawyer feel superior. He is a member of an elite inner circle, unlike the

None of the Above ☑

ordinary citizen who must be content with membership in a lower social order. The lawyer holds the keys to the castle in the inaccessible kingdom of law.

This feeling of elitism blossoms in law school and reaches maturity after the lawyer enters practice. It is reinforced when the lawyer comes into contact with people facing serious problems who feel totally inadequate to deal with the law themselves and must therefore place their future in his hands. This easily generates a feeling of power in the lawyer, as he sees himself a part of an intellectual vanguard, able to decipher and manipulate complex legalistic jargon.

Such behavior is not new to the human species; the lawyer may think of himself as an advancement in the evolutionary scale, but in fact he is something of an anachronism.

Thousands of years ago, primitive tribes relied upon the Shaman, or witch doctor, to protect them from evil forces, to assist and prescribe the necessary rituals and sacrifices to pacify the various gods of rain, sunshine, hunting, love, peace, war, or anything else that the tribespeople viewed as important to their survival and well-being. These "needs" were considered by the tribal members as outside of their area of understanding and control, so it was fortunate that someone

None of the Above ☑

"chosen" would be among them to act as interpreter-protector.

In order to maintain their image, the witch doctors adorned themselves with a variety of objects — some for beauty, but mostly to inspire fear and an awesome respect that brought blind obedience. Grotesque masks, feathers, furs, skin dyes, and body-distorting appendages were designed to impress the tribe with their unique and supernatural powers. The witch doctors also employed special languages, along with the symbols and tokens which were not to be questioned or touched by the common people.

So whenever the tribe was in need of something or other (and that was probably a perpetual condition), they would place the problem before the witch doctor and he would intercede in their behalf. If the results were more or less satisfactory, the Shaman's power was still effective and he was allowed to continue "practicing." If he suffered a serious failure and could not explain it adequately, he was then "disbarred" from future practice either by banishment from the tribe or something more direct, such as lopping off his head.

I, personally, would be willing to venture that today's lawyers can trace their methods back to the ancient witch doctors and their suppliant tribespeople. After all, there has been little sig-

None of the Above ☑

nificant change. Today's legal practitioners still carry a bag of magical powders, incense, and bird feathers — it's called a law library. And today's Shamans claim an elitist relationship with the god of law, the source of all justice and knowledge whose final decisions must never be challenged. The penalty for disobeying this god is banishment from the tribe — or death.

While the practice (law) and its practitioners (lawyers) have developed their mystique to a fine point of effectiveness, the rank and file members of society have made virtually no progress in their general attitude toward today's witch doctors.

Their "medicine" is so powerful that we are not only victimized by them, we are *willingly* victimized.

Lawyers comprise a secret fraternity replete with passwords and rituals. Everything must sound technical and official, and the brothers and sisters share a secret code. There are no questions in Legaland, there are "interrogatories." There are no statements, just "depositions." Papers are not signed, they are "executed." (Are they blindfolded first?) Do lawyers interview prospective jurors? Never — that would be too intelligible. They *"voir dire"* the jury. Add to these a long list of other technical terms, many in Latin (which even the Catholic Church doesn't insist on using anymore), and you have a secret code for grown-

None of the Above ☑

ups. A kid deciphers the secret code on the back of a Wheaties box with a super-secret spy ring. His adult counterpart, the lawyer, is a bit more sophisticated. He's completed the initiation (known as "passing the bar"), has a degree, gets paid, and — most distressing of all — is taken seriously by his peers.

Lawyers have a vested interest in maintaining the religious mumbo jumbo of law. The more incomprehensible the legal procedures, the more absolute faith must be placed in the lawyer's powers. The lawyer will not question the sanctity of the law. It is Holy Scripture, it is truth, honesty, reality, the foundation of civilized society. Should you point out to the lawyer that totalitarian societies have more laws than any others, you'll probably be brushed aside with an impatient glance, since you've dared to trespass upon the Holy Ground which is beyond your ability to comprehend.

Further intensifying the lawyer's elitism are the rituals of a courtroom, many of which center around a judge. A judge, in plain fact, is just a lawyer who's advanced in the hierarchy. A judge is to a lawyer as a bishop is to a priest. Like the bishop, the judge is somberly attired. He must be paid homage; people must rise when he enters the room, and address him as "Your Honor." He is elevated above the rest of the courtroom, pre-

None of the Above ☑

sumably because that puts him in closer touch with "higher powers." And where else in the United States today, except in a courtroom, can you be prosecuted for blasphemy? Should you blaspheme the judge — should you insult him in some way or use language that offends his sensibilities — you'll end up paying a fine or possibly spending time in jail for "contempt of court." To insult a judge is to attack society itself. He is the symbol of honor and justice, the sacred (if cloudy and undefined) tenets of our state-religion. No church ever had it so good — or so powerful.

The lawyer has an uncanny ability to make everything complex beyond belief. If you go to a lawyer with a simple problem, rest assured that he will transform it into a complicated monstrosity. As legal technicalities increase, the lawyer becomes more indispensable. If a married couple consults a lawyer for a divorce on amiable terms, he will usually refer one of them to another lawyer. This, he will say, is to protect the interests of both parties. Another reason, however, is that if he handles both sides, he cannot benefit by setting them at each other's throats in disputes over property settlement, child custody, etc. If another lawyer is involved, the husband can be pitted against the wife and vice versa. What could have been a brief, amiable separation turns into a legal brawl where feelings are hurt and friendships are

None of the Above ☑

irreparably damaged. To the lawyers, it is simply another exercise in the profitable game of law where, even if they lose, someone else feels the crunch.

Since lawyers enjoy this power and prestige, it is not surprising that law attracts power-hungry, authoritarian personalities — the stuff from which politicians are made. You may think that we are a nation of laws and not of men — but think again. *Who* makes the laws? Men do, of course — more specifically, lawyers-turned-politicians make the laws. The legal profession is not simply a passive victim of incomprehensible and arbitrary law; the law did not come from heaven inscribed on tablets of stone. A special branch of the legal profession — the political wing — is responsible for those laws. *Lawyers make the law, and lawyers benefit through its enforcement.* Never before has a single profession so effectively created a demand for its own services! And remember, this demand is created forcibly, not through voluntary agreement.

Furthermore, there is no single group in the country — except lawyers — that is allowed to police itself; lawyers aren't answerable to a government agency, they need not be concerned with "truth in packaging" or even licenses. They've got what criminals call "a perfect con" — it's so complicated that no one can tell whether they're doing it right or wrong. If an architect designs a leaning tower, it's no secret. But let a lawyer write a contract with angles and loopholes and errors of omission, and who's to know except another lawyer? To paraphrase Mark Twain, a burglar couldn't do it better.

Where do we begin to set things right? As a first step, remove the special interest group from politics; do not permit lawyers to hold political office. *Lawyers should be barred from holding public office.* This would have many beneficial effects. First, it would leave politicians no choice but to make the law intelligible, since without legal training they could not understand it themselves if it were not. Second, it would sever the family ties between politicians and lawyers. Instead of acting as apologists for one another, they could develop a healthy sense of mutual distrust and act as watchdogs over each other. Finally, if lawyers could not become politicians, much of the power-lust incentive would be removed from law and it would attract a more civilized breed of persons. Thus, instead of forever defending the legal status quo, lawyers might begin to think and to question. After all, they'd have no alternative but to defend people against injustice — instead of defending unjust laws at the expense of people.

None of the Above ☑
___

Chapter 9

Principles Are Practical

    Defenders of freedom are often charged with being too wrapped up in principles, with being too theoretical and idealistic; and they are admonished to come down to the hardheaded, everyday world of facts, where "things just aren't that simple." To be concerned with the principle of freedom is to be labeled at best, a dreamer, and at worst, a fool.

    But what are those who pit principles against facts really saying? Do these people understand principles, freedom, and their roles in human life? In some cases there is a lack of proper understanding, but some enemies of freedom do understand the issues involved, which is why they fight against them so energetically.

    Every person acts on the basis of principles. There is no escaping this. Just being alive requires that you make choices — hundreds of them everyday. You may not be consciously aware of every choice you make, such as when you decide what to eat, what to wear, when to sit, what to say and so forth; but you are constantly making decisions

None of the Above ☑

of one kind or another. How are these decisions made? Obviously in most instances you don't sit down, draw up a list of alternatives and then select the best one. This is impossible because it involves too much time and effort. When you are deciding what to eat, you cannot run through a list of every food in existence and then select from that list. When you are deciding how to spend your time for a day, you cannot consider every possible alternative, such as driving to any one of a thousand cities, and then select one of the possibilities. If you attempted to do this, you would spend your entire day just considering the possibilities and you would never get around to doing anything.

Here we have an apparent problem. We must make countless decisions in our lives, yet we are not able to consider every possibility open to us. How, then, do we make decisions? With the aid of *principles*. Principles are our means of discriminating and selecting among the thousands of options available to us. Principles clarify our goals and enable us to be in control of our lives. Principles are an indispensable tool for making intelligent, knowledgeable decisions, and anyone who attacks principles is actually attacking our ability to choose. Anyone who says, "Don't take principles too seriously," is really saying, "Don't worry about making intelligent choices." And

None of the Above ☑

what does this mean, if not, "Don't worry about your own life and happiness"?

Let's take a closer look at how principles enable us to make choices. A principle is simply a generalized statement of fact. If I say I have two eyes, I am making a particular statement about myself which, although true, is not a principle. If however, I say that all humans normally have two eyes, I am giving a principle, a general truth, about humans. Similarly, if I say I am not going to vote in the next election, this statement, although true, is not a principle. But if I say, "Since elections do not provide a true choice, I am not going to participate in them," this is a principle, a general truth, about my plan of action.

So it is obvious that all of us have principles. We all have general plans of action on which we base our lives. These plans include such things as our long- and short-term goals, our desires for what we want out of life, our ideas about what things give us pleasure, the kinds of friends we want, what distinguishes right from wrong and so on. These are the principles on which we act in situations of choice. When I get up in the morning, I don't have to consider every action open to me. Because I know generally what I want to do, because I have a life plan, my alternatives are narrowed down to a reasonable level. Maybe I have some pressing business that requires attention, So

I'll concentrate on that, but I certainly won't consider the option (although I could if I wanted to) of becoming a plumber's apprentice or a politician.

Principles, therefore, bring order and management to our lives. We all act on the basis of principles, whether we like it or not. The only way to escape principles would be to stop making choices, and the only way to accomplish this would be to stop living. Some people, of course, have "better" principles than others; principles that are more efficient, more consistent or more realistic. Although we don't have control over *whether* we act on principles, we do have control over the quality of our principles. We do have control over whether our principles will work for our benefit and happiness.

Now what is the real message of the political mentality when it tells us that we are too concerned with principles; especially the principle of free choice? This is not a plea to abandon principles altogether, which would be impossible; instead it is a plea to abandon the principle that the political mentality finds annoying and uncomfortable: the principal that stands between what *we* want to do and what the *politician* wants us to do. In other words, the politician does not like the principle of freedom because if people adopted it consistently he would be minus a lucrative job. So

None of the Above ☑

he bids us to give up this principle, which he labels "unrealistic" or "utopian." Meanwhile, he attempts to substitute his own principle — that we should let the politician make our important decisions for us.

When the political mentality says that the person who upholds the principle of freedom is "unrealistic," what is meant is that it is unrealistic to suppose that you are able to run your own life; it is unrealistic to suppose that you are able to make intelligent decisions by yourself. Then comes the clincher: the politician will make those decisions for you. He is more intelligent than you; he knows what you "really" want and what will "really" make you happy. In the name of being more realistic and more concerned with hard-headed facts, we are supposed to accept this nonsense. We are supposed to grant the politician a near-omniscience, and we are supposed to turn control of our lives over to him on this assumption. Something more unrealistic can hardly be imagined.

Now some people may decide they don't like the responsibility of making important decisions, and they may choose to turn this responsibility over to the politician. That is their privilege. But most Americans undoubtedly do not wish to have control over their lives pre-empted in this manner. Most Americans are not about to put their future happiness in the slippery hands of a politician. But the politicians are wresting more and more control from us nonetheless. And as that sphere of control increases, *our* sphere of control, our ability to manage our own lives, *decreases*.

For those of us who wish to regain autonomy over our lives, the principle of freedom is crucial. It is the best way to assert that we don't want the politician telling us what to do, that we are competent human beings who are perfectly able to run our own lives. So the next time the political mentality tells you that you are too enamored with principles and that you should be more "realistic," beware! Look closely at what he is trying to deprive you of and what he aims to put in its place. The politician is attempting to strip you of your right to choose, to substitute his choices and desires for yours. The political attack on principles is merely a subterfuge to substitute the principle of force for that of free choice.

___*None of the Above* ☑___

Chapter 10

What Is Your Freedom Worth?

How much would you take in exchange for your freedom? If you were offered a comfortable home, plenty of food, sufficient diversion and entertainment, etc., with the stipulation that your life will be planned by someone else, that another person will make your decisions for you which you will be required to obey, would you accept the offer? Few people would, for they recognize that a slave, no matter how comfortable, is still a slave. Most of us realize that it is essential to our happiness that we be able to act on our own value judgments rather than following the dictates of someone else. It is a cliché, but it is true, that wealth alone does not bring happiness. Some people with low or moderate incomes are happier than those of wealth. Essential to happiness is the right to choose for ourselves; and regardless of the material rewards dangled in front of us, it would be a mistake — indeed, a disaster — to sacrifice this right for something else.

You might argue that you would give up your freedom in exchange for a million dollars. But you

None of the Above ☑

are probably visualizing how you would spend the million dollars, which misses the point of the original question. Sure, you will be given a million dollars, and it will be spent on you one way or another, but since you have given up your right to choose, you will have no say in how it is spent. If your benefactor decides you should live on a yacht but you are deathly afraid of water, too bad. You have relinquished your freedom, and you must live on the yacht, like a seasick millionaire. If your benefactor decides that it is in your interest to be cultured and that you should therefore become a classical pianist but you hate classical music, too bad. You will be forced to learn the piano, and you will be a cultured, though desperately unhappy, millionaire pianist. If you enjoy watching TV westerns but your benefactor deems them too violent for you, you can say goodbye to your favorite cowboy, for you have seen your last TV western.

The moral here is that even money is useless without the right to spend it as you see fit. This is why it is impossible to put a price on freedom. Without freedom to choose, everything, including money, loses its value.

You might think that you would be willing to sell your freedom if only the purchaser, your benefactor, will give you what you want anyway. If what you really want to do is travel around the

None of the Above ☑

world for the rest of your life, why not give up your freedom in exchange for a life of travel? If a person promises everything you would choose on your own anyway, why not give up your freedom in exchange?

This offer assumes a degree of predictability that is in fact not present. First, although you may know in general terms what you want, it is impossible to specify down to the last iota what your future desires will be. Suppose, as a world traveler, you want to go to France, so your benefactor sends you there. Upon arriving you find that you don't like France after all and you want to leave. But your benefactor may decide otherwise and you will be stuck with his decision. After you are in France, how will you want to spend your days? It is impossible to say in advance, so what you will do after you reach France will again be a matter for your benefactor to decide.

Because our values are constantly shifting and changing, there is no way to say with certainty what the future holds in store for us. By selling your freedom for the satisfaction of present wants, you leave the remainder of your life "up for grabs" and place yourself totally at the mercy of your benefactor.

In addition, after your benefactor has control over your life, you have no way to guarantee that he'll carry through with his part of the bargain.

None of the Above ☑

Once you have given him power over you, you cannot choose to take it back because your right of choice is the very thing you relinquished. You are in the iron grip of your benefactor.

No matter how we look at it, then, to sell your freedom is a bad bargain. It is almost the same as selling your life. Of what use would money or physical possessions be to you if you were dead? There would be, in fact, no "you" to enjoy these things. Similarly, the kind of person you are, your character and personality, are an expression of your values and choices. If you are deprived of your choices you cannot act to fulfill your values, and there is no longer a psychological "you" who is capable of enjoying happiness. You become a mere physical object, a robot, totally within the control of someone else. Just as killing yourself is physical suicide, so selling your freedom is psychological suicide.

Now what is the point of this discussion? Even if someone offered to buy your freedom outright, which is unlikely, you probably would not sell it. But the point is that many people are selling their freedom today, and — what is even more distressing — they are selling it for peanuts. To whom are they selling their freedom? To the politicians.

The government, our politicians tell us, will provide us with education, health care, food, or any number of other necessities. Of course, the

None of the Above ☑

government does no such thing, since it does not produce anything but merely spends money acquired from us through taxation. But overlooking this for the moment, what are we supposed to give up in return for these benefits? The answer is clear: We are supposed to give up our right to choose.

The government, through the use of tax monies, may supply public schools, but we no longer have a choice as to educational content and standards. The government now decides what is appropriate to teach our children and by what methods it will be taught. We can send our children to private schools, but even these must be accredited by the government. And this is assuming that parents can afford a private school after the government has siphoned off a substantial percentage of their income into the public school system. Worst of all, a child is forced by law to attend school until a certain age, perhaps against the wishes of the child and the parents. Thus, in the name of education, which could be provided perfectly well without government interference, Americans sell a measure of their freedom to choose.

The same holds true in other areas of government intervention. The government may provide you with medical care but it will tell you which doctors you may go to. If your doctor is not properly recognized, you are out of luck. And the government will tell you which drugs you may and may not take. If it decides to outlaw a particular substance (which some people, rightly or wrongly, claim as a cure for cancer), you can become a criminal merely by attempting to exercise freedom of choice.

So the alleged benefits provided by government are paid for at a high price: we must give up our right to choose. But isn't it true that some of the goods and services provided by government are so essential and indispensable that they are worth at least some of our freedom in exchange? Some people may decide this is the case, and they are free to bargain away their freedom. But many of us do not consider the trade to be a good one, and we prefer to retain our right of choice. We realize that, although some of the goods and services provided by government are essential, *it is not essential that they be provided by government*. On the contrary, the private marketplace, operating on the principle of voluntary cooperation and exchange, is not only able to provide these goods and services but can provide them more efficiently and for less money.

In every area where the politician interferes with your life, he wishes to restrict your range of choice and thereby deprive you of some of your freedom. If he simply laid his cards on the table and said, "I want to give you orders," he would be

None of the Above ☑

ignored or despised. So he comes bearing gifts. "I will give you education, or food, or housing," he says, "and all you have to do is give me some control over your life. Let me make the important decisions for you, and I will reward you." At times the politician may actually deliver on his promises, if for no other reason than to keep his credibility; but usually, after he is in power he goes his merry way. At this point he is difficult to stop because after sacrificing their autonomy the people who elected him to office are deprived of any means by which to hold him in check.

We must always remember that choice is subjective. We choose on the basis of our subjective evaluations, and no one has a right to force upon us their idea of what is good for us. Others may try to persuade us of our errors, but the final decision rests with the individual. Since I believe that to sell your freedom is unwise, I will attempt to persuade you that to trade away your freedom to politicians in exchange for alleged benefits is a dangerous decision with potentially devastating consequences. But, in the final analysis, you must decide for yourself, and I will not interfere with your decision.

By the same token, however, I want to be able to decide for myself whether or not to sell my freedom, and I want to do so without interference from others. Personally, my freedom to choose is

None of the Above ☑

priceless because without this right all other values are meaningless. My autonomy is indispensable to my happiness. Therefore, when the politician promises me more happiness in exchange for my autonomy, I know he is either misguided or lying. Even if I came out ahead in material goods, even if selling my freedom made me rich, I would have bargained away the very means by which to enjoy those riches. The value of material wealth lies in its capacity to expand my range of choices. If in order to gain wealth I must *constrict* my range of choices, I sabotage my own efforts to attain happiness.

Thus, no price can be put on freedom. Politicians, who spend most of their time and energy negotiating for the freedom of other people, are little more than carnival hucksters who must swagger and bluster in their efforts to camouflage what is, in the end, a rotten deal.

None of the Above ☑

Chapter 11

Freedom In The Balance

We often hear it said that life is a series of compromises; that in order to get along in the world we must be willing to give as well as take. If we are to get what we want, we must give up something in exchange. This trading process is essential to our way of life. We can't expect to get things free, and we can't expect to get things without the cooperation of other people, so we must be willing to negotiate with others, and sometimes bend a little if we are to maintain our well-being.

This observation, although true, can be misleading when applied to freedom of choice. Politicians continually remark, when passing a new law that restricts individual liberty, that the loss of freedom is being "exchanged for" or "balanced by" other benefits. (These alleged benefits, of course, usually turn out to benefit the politicians and their supporters.) So, if we believe the politicians, we are merely exchanging one thing for another — a slice of freedom is being traded for other advantages. There is nothing unusual about

None of the Above ☑

this, the politicians assure us, since this kind of thing occurs all the time. It is part of the give and take of life.

If you don't raise your eyebrows at this suspicious bit of reasoning, you should. For unlike other exchanges, *we* are not deciding to trade our freedom for something else; the politician is making the choice for us. But you cannot trade something that belongs to someone else. In presuming that he has the right to bargain with our freedom, the politician assumes that he controls our right to choose in the first place, and that he can trade this right itself at his discretion. To grant this assumption is to make us virtual slaves of the politician, and the battle is lost before it is even begun.

In addition, an exchange requires that you desire and choose that which is being offered in trade. If you buy a cow for $100, it is because you desire the cow more than the money. Conversely, the person who sells you the cow desires the money more than the cow or else he would not participate in the exchange.

This is the motive that leads to trade. If person A has something that person B wants, and B has something that A wants, they may reach an agreement to trade. They may trade directly or they may barter, or they may use a more sophisticated version of monetary exchange. But regardless of

None of the Above ☑

the mechanics, the basic principle remains unchanged. Both parties give up something in exchange for something they want more, and hence both parties benefit. Both persons attain values because they get something they desire more than that which they had previously. Thus, if A gives B a cow in exchange for a horse, A must have valued the horse more than the cow or he would not have participated in the exchange. Therefore, he benefits, he attains a value by getting the horse.

Essential to this process of exchange is the subjective valuation by all parties concerned that they are benefiting by the exchange. An exchange that you are forced to accept is meaningless nonsense. If someone takes something from you forcibly, even if he gives you something back, you are the victim of a robbery, not a participant in an exchange.

But this is precisely what happens when the politician allegedly trades your freedom for something else. If the politician has such a great offer, why doesn't he present it to you and then let you decide? He doesn't do this, of course, because you will probably refuse. So he decides for you. He forces an "exchange" upon you whether you want it or not. He will take your money and your freedom to choose, and he may, if you are lucky, give you something back. But since you had no choice in the matter, this is not an exchange of

None of the Above ☑

any kind. It is robbery, and the unjust usurpation of your autonomy, pure and simple.

What if the politician gives you something back that is really valuable? Doesn't this change things? No, not at all. We must ask: valuable to *whom*? Whatever the politician is offering cannot be that valuable to you because you are unwilling to trade for it voluntarily. Now the politician may think that you *should* value what he is offering you — indeed, he will call you everything from "unpatriotic" to "apathetic" in an effort to make you feel guilty for not valuing it — but here he is trying to impose his idea of how you should live. So let's call a spade a spade. The business of the politician is to meddle in your affairs and to tell you how you should live. Any talk of "balancing" the loss of your freedom by exchanging it for other benefits is just so much hot air.

Perhaps the "benefits" offered by the politician are of value to some people. Fine; then let them negotiate with the politician, let them trade away their freedom, but leave the rest of us out of it. Our freedom is not theirs to bargain with.

Whenever the politician speaks of exchanging freedom — the right to choose — for something else, he treats freedom as if it were just another commodity on an equal footing with other commodities such as cars and bicycles. Thus, he tells us, it is just a matter of simple exchange; of giving up one commodity for another. But this is a false picture. Freedom is not a commodity; rather, it is a condition among humans where force is absent. Freedom is the general framework in which human choice and cooperation are possible. Take away choice and cooperation, and exchange is no longer possible. Freedom is a necessary condition for the process of exchange. Therefore, to deprive a person of his freedom is to deprive him of his ability to exchange *anything*.

This is why freedom is not just another commodity and why it is extremely dangerous to talk about "exchanging" freedom for something else. To trade your freedom to the politician is to lessen control over your life and to place that control in the hands of the politician. As your autonomy deteriorates more and more, you decrease your ability to choose, and thereby undercut your right to exchange with others. The less you are able to choose, the less you are in control of your actions, and to that degree you are not a free agent in the position to trade with others on an equal footing. Instead, you become a dupe of political power seekers who presume to make your choices for you.

This does not mean that some people will never choose to surrender their freedom. Unfortunately, some people do. But you should at least be aware of what is at stake. Every time you let more of

None of the Above ☑

your freedom slip away, or every time you "exchange" a bit of your freedom for a political benefit (as many special interest groups do), you are contributing to the destruction of your own autonomy. You are contributing to a process that will eventually engulf you, as you find one day that your right to choose has eroded to such an extent that politicians are controlling virtually every area of your life. And then it will be too late.

None of the Above ☑

Chapter 12

A Gang By Any Other Name...

Political parties, along with their jargon and hoopla, have long been a part of the American political scene. Even today, when no one really believes that campaign promises and party platforms have much to do with what the politician will do once in office, there still remains an aura of goodness and right around the idea of political parties and their sacred function. But if you strip away the jargon and take a hard look at what political parties actually do, you get a picture entirely different from the one we grew up with in the civics books.

When it comes right down to it, political parties deal in power. A party is a group of people trying to amass as much power as possible so they can implement their ideas of how we all should live. In exchange for giving the party our support, the party promises us jobs, health care, protection from all manner of evils and the knowledge that we are in the right because we chose the "good guys" to rule us. The exchange is simple — we give them power and support through our votes and money, and they give us protection from real or imaginary evils. The whole process is legitimized with the rhetoric of civic duty, maintaining the two-party system and participatory democracy.

But consider another kind of group whose functions and promises are similar to those of political parties. This kind of group, however, does not have centuries of ready-made slogans to make it palatable to the public, nor does it have the sanction of society and the law. No, this powerful group operates outside of the law, and it is called a "gang," not a political party.

At first glance, it may seem absurd to compare political parties to gangs. After all, we know that gang activities are illegal whereas political activities are not. But if we look closely at the structure, function and purpose of political parties and gangs, we find that, except for a difference in terminology, they are in many ways the same kind of organization.

Let's examine the similarities: A political party is a group of people trying to amass as much power as possible so they can implement their ideas of how we all should live. This is also true of a gang. Both a political party and a gang depend on power to put their ideas and goals into practice. A gang offers you the use of its power as protection in return for your money, cooperation and favors. If you don't pay for the "protection,"

None of the Above ☑

your property may be destroyed or you may be beaten up. When in power, a political party offers you "protection" in exchange for your money (taxes), and if you don't pay, your property is confiscated and you may wind up in jail.

With either group — gang or party — you pay one way or another whether you like it or not. When someone takes something that doesn't belong to them by force, we call it stealing. When a gang steals, no one is confused about what to call it; when the party in power steals your money, it's called taxation. But just as you can't change the nature of a skunk by defining it as a striped pussycat with a pungent aroma, neither can you change the nature of stealing by calling it taxation and by defining it as a voluntary, patriotic means of raising revenue. To argue that the political party's "tax" provides for some good and necessary service does not alter the fact that the acquisition process was one of theft. During the 1930s supporters of Adolph Hitler pointed to the many hospitals, social services and magnificent highways that were the product of his regime. So we see that both the gang and the political party in power finance their activities in the same way — by stealing. First, they try to convince the people to give support willingly. When that fails or is insufficient, they take whatever they consider necessary by force or the threat of force.

None of the Above ☑

It may be said that an important difference between the gang and the political party is that, in primaries and general elections, we choose our bosses in the political party but we have no such choice of gang leaders. We are told that primaries are public activities, but it's more accurate to say that primaries are political activities which take place in public — and that is a very different story. It leaves us, the public, without any real say in who the "leaders" will be. By the time the general elections roll around, the only choice we have is which gang — the Democrats or the Republicans — will have more power. There is no real choice here. And those who are disenchanted with the alternatives are charged with "apathy," "lack of responsibility" or "idealism," in an attempt at intimidation.

Some claim that the two-party system is highly efficient and that to give the voters more than two choices would become unwieldy. But employing that logic, a dictatorship is even more efficient than a two-party system and hence more desirable. It just depends on what you want. If a gang is out to kill you, would you feel better knowing that the gang has thoughtfully and efficiently lifted the cumbersome burden of choice from you as to whether or not you want to stay alive?

And what is more important: The hallmark of a self-governing society is free choice. When free

None of the Above ☑

choice is "reasoned" into a secondary position and replaced with little or no choice, what is left is a system of slavery. We end up discussing the degree of slavery we will tolerate rather than whether we will be free or unfree.

Because the nature of their game is power, it is a safe bet that those who make it to the top in gangs are the most powerful. And as we have seen many times in political scandal, powerful men rarely possess the virtues of honesty, integrity and moral courage. It has been said that power corrupts and that absolute power corrupts absolutely. It would be more accurate to say that only the absolutely corrupt seek absolute power. If someone comes to you and asks for the power to run your life, or to run the lives of other people, chances are good that he is not to be trusted and that turning your back on him is a risky venture.

It is not mere coincidence that both political leaders and gang leaders travel with an entourage of advance men and bodyguards. Both kinds of bosses realize that just as they inflict violence on others (if not directly, then by decree), so some people may attempt to retaliate by inflicting violence on them. It is interesting to note that political bosses who proclaim themselves the "people's choice" are as nervous for their safety as are the gangland chiefs who make no pretense about being the choice of the public. One difference between

None of the Above ☑

gang leaders and political leaders, then, is that gang leaders are less devious.

There is another difference: gang members are generally less meddlesome than politicians. Sometimes they simply take your money and run. Politicians, on the other hand, take your money and then insist on running you. At least the gangster has the decency to leave you alone much of the time; he does not presume to be your benefactor or your protector; he does not insist that you praise him and call him "Sir." He does not claim to represent you. No, the gangster does not inflict these absurdities upon you. He does not, in addition to robbing you, insult your intelligence. But not so the politicians. After taking your money, which is bad enough, the politician will not go away and leave you alone. He insists on "serving" you whether you want his services or not. And if you oppose him or attempt to ignore him, you may be labeled with anything from "apathetic" to "unpatriotic" and "dangerous."

Despite these differences, however, political parties and gangs are cut from the same cloth. Their functions and means of financing are practically identical. Now some people may want the services of politicians and political parties, just as some people want the services of a gang; this depends on what your goals are and how much violence you are willing to tolerate to achieve them.

None of the Above ☑

But at least we could eliminate much confusion by using the same terms to describe both organizations. When a political party threatens violence if they are not given money, then let's call it extortion, not taxation. If a politician conscripts you into his gang (the army), let's call this involuntary servitude by its proper names — kidnapping and slavery. If these activities are really as essential as politicians would like us to believe, then they shouldn't need to be camouflaged in doubletalk. And if it turns out that such practices, when correctly identified, are less popular as a result — well, that is good to know, too.

Chapter 13

Are Non-Voters Apathetic?

> "History, from the earliest Christians downward, is full of instances of men who refused all connection with government and all the influences which office could bestow rather than deny their principles or aid in wrongdoing. Sir Thomas More need never have mounted the scaffold, had he only consented to take the oath of supremacy. He had only to tell a lie with solemnity, as we are asked to do, and he might not only have saved his life, but, as the trimmers of his day would have told him, doubled his influence. Pitt resigned his place as Prime Minister of England rather than break faith with the Catholics of Ireland. Should I not resign a ballot rather than break faith with the slave?"
>
> — Wendell Phillips
> Rudolph Rocker,
> *Pioneers of American Freedom*
> 1949

An ever-increasing number of Americans are refusing to go to the polls on election day. It looks as if millions of people are coming to the conclusion that it just isn't worth the effort. This attitude is quite understandable in these times of broken campaign promises and the "credibility gap" (as political lying is so politely called). What

None of the Above ☑

good does it do to vote for a politician when you know that there is about as much chance of him doing what he says after he is in office as there is of a mugger taking just one dollar if you offer him your wallet? Many people are concluding that to vote with the present system is futile.

Americans have long been proud of their hard-headed realism and practicality. The present voter attitude of boredom and skepticism toward politicians, the suspicion that politicians will continue their tired song-and-dance routine to the tune of Yankee Doodle, is just another instance of American realism. And given the actions of politicians in the past, this is a very understandable and healthy attitude.

What is not understandable, however, is how anyone could level the charge of irresponsibility or apathy at a non-voter who refuses to participate in a farce at the polls. We have been lied to and hoodwinked time and again; we have watched our taxes skyrocket to pay for the boondoggles and pet projects of politicians who promise to lower taxes. Is it any wonder, after we have been kicked around and cheated so many times, that we are reluctant to be kicked around and cheated some more?

Who is calling the non-voting public irresponsible and apathetic? Not surprisingly, it is the politicians — the same politicians who spin fairy

None of the Above ☑

tales at election time and who then get upset when few people care which king of nonsense gets elected, be he an elephant or a donkey. Your local grocer would be laughed out of business if he whined that his customers were "apathetic" because they refused to buy his rotten bananas. But the politician whines in the same way when he charges people with apathy because they won't buy his rotten promises.

If you strip away the rhetoric, all the politician really says when he charges the non-voting public with apathy is that the non-voters won't do what he wants them to do — namely, give him support and money. Politicians need money to finance campaigns, and they need votes so they can present themselves as the "people's choice," thereby passing off their deeds as the "will of the people." Thus it is understandable that politicians concocted the term "apathy" to distort the unpleasant fact that not many people want them in office. As voting day statistics get gloomier and gloomier, their minds must work overtime to invent new excuses that shift the blame from themselves to the non-voters.

Politicians have been somewhat successful in clouding the issues — in lending some plausibility to the nonsense that non-voters are "un-American," or "irresponsible," or that at least non-voters deserve by default whoever is elected and whatever they do while in office. This last is an especially strange twist of logic; it is akin to saying that, if a mob is voting whether to shoot or to hang John Jones, and if John Jones refuses the mob's invitation to cast his vote for one or the other, and if the mob decides on hanging, John Jones (by default) thereby deserves to hang. Obviously, John Jones doesn't want to hang or to be shot; he is not apathetic because he refuses to vote for one or the other. He doesn't vote because he doesn't want either of the alternatives offered to him — he dislikes both intensely — and this is a far cry from being indifferent.

It never occurs to the politicians that perhaps the non-voters, like John Jones, don't want *any* of the alternatives offered to them at the polls; and that this, rather than apathy or indifference, is the reason they don't vote. In one sense, of course, non-voters are indifferent; since they see no genuine alternatives listed on the ballot, they don't care much whether politician A or politician B gets elected. But many non-voters do have strong opinions and preferences — they would like to say "No" to all of the politicians on the ballot.

Many non-voters see abstention at the polls as the only avenue by which they can register their dissatisfaction; they simply refuse to sanction a voting farce where they are offered no real choice.

None of the Above ☑

It is high time that politicians realized that just as people don't buy when they don't like what is being sold, so they don't vote when they don't like who is running for office. When Ford Motors' Edsel didn't sell, they didn't accuse the car buyers of apathy toward Edsels. Instead, they realized that people were not buying because they didn't like the product, and they took it off the market. But politicians are still trying to sell us Edsels (themselves); they are still trying to pass themselves off as responsible leaders admired by the public. And when the voting public doesn't respond, the people get blamed, not the politicians. But suppose, just suppose, that the non-voters are communicating the same message to politicians that the non-buyers communicated to Ford Motors; i.e., "We don't like what you're selling and we want nothing to do with it." This hardly qualifies as apathy.

People often turn away from the polls in confusion because they feel frustrated and used, and because they don't know what else to do. But a voters' boycott should become a conscious, explicit position, so it will communicate to politicians the widespread dissatisfaction among people. Non-voting here is a conscious, responsible position to adopt — indeed, it is the only responsible position to adopt for a voter who cannot find someone or something *positive* to vote *for*.

None of the Above ☑

When you vote, you are supposed to be choosing a capable person to represent you for years to come. To choose wisely, you must be abreast of the issues — the candidates' qualifications and their records of performance. Then, taking these facts into consideration, you choose the best candidate. What is assumed here, of course, is that there is a "best man," that at least one person among the candidates deserves your respect and confidence. But, more and more often, you find that you don't respect or trust any of the candidates. There is, for you, no "best man," only a motley crew reminiscent of anything from the Three Stooges to Attila the Hun. In such a case you have no real choice, and the alleged purpose of voting is destroyed. To choose among two or more evils is presumably not what voting is supposed to be about.

Many non-voters are concerned, responsible people who want nothing to do with the present election-day circus. But these voters would like to make themselves heard. At present all they can do is stay away from the polls. If, however, a "None of the Above is Acceptable" option were put on all ballots, the non-voters could become voters — they could vote "No" on all the candidates.

Until this option is available, however, the only way to say "No" to the political mobs and their con men is to refuse to vote, and to make it clear

None of the Above ☑

to all concerned *why* you are refusing to vote. Politicians would like us to believe that non-voters are copping out, but the truth is just the opposite. To accede to an electoral process that offers only an illusion of choice, *to choose the lesser of two evils, is the real cop-out.*

This is still a relatively free country and free people have a right to say "No." This is the essence of the right to choose. Beware of anyone who tells you that your "No" represents apathy; chances are good that he wishes to deprive you of your inherent right to choose.

None of the Above ☑

Chapter 14

Choice: The Third Alternative

> "*I heartily accept the motto — 'That government is best which governs least'; and I should like to see it acted up to more rapidly and systematically. Carried out it finally amounts to this, which I also believe, — 'That government is best which governs not at all,' and when men are prepared for it, that will be the kind of government they will have.*"
>
> Henry David Thoreau
> *On the Duty of Civil Disobedience,*
> 1849

Politicians are forever telling us how to spend our money and how to lead our lives. They are especially aggressive in election years when they are competing for power. Although the issues they argue are unclear, one thing *is* clear: each competitor is convinced that he is best fit to rule. But however much they disagree about the best man for the job, politicians are unanimous when it comes to implementing their ideas. Force is the political way. Political controversies narrow down not to whether force should be used (which is assumed without question), but who is going to wield the force and how. The only choice we have

None of the Above ☑

at the polls is which politician is going to do the forcing. There is a third alternative, however, that is rarely considered: this is to expel force from our lives and to run our own affairs.

As things now stand, politicians do not compete for a chance to help us maximize control over our lives; for, as we gain control, they lose power. And you can hardly expect a politician to give up power, any more than you can expect a baboon to give up bananas. But just because politicians are reluctant to leave us alone doesn't mean that opting for more choice and control in our lives is not a worthwhile goal. Given the nature of human beings, free choice is so crucial to our happiness that we must never give up the struggle to attain and keep it.

Human beings must act in order to live, and choice is a prerequisite for action. Action requires that we choose among the millions of different alternatives open to us. If we did not choose, we would be paralyzed by indecision. Think of how many choices you have to make just to get out of bed. First, you have to decide what time to set the alarm for, and then you have to decide how to respond after it rings. Are you going to turn it off and go back to sleep? Are you going to throw it against the wall? Or are you going to jump up and get out of bed? Your choice of action is determined by your goal. If your goal is to get to

None of the Above ☑

work on time, chances are you will get out of bed. But if you are on vacation, you may choose to shut the alarm off and go back to sleep. Or if your goal is to vent your pent-up frustrations, you may throw the clock against the wall. Which action is right, in any situation, depends upon your goal. And to choose wisely you must have confidence in your ability to take actions that will help achieve your goals.

This confidence is gained by making judgments, acting on them, and seeing if they accomplish the ends we want. This is part of what it means to be an adult. Maturation is a process of extending our range of choices and gaining more control over our lives. When we were children, our parents made most of our important decisions for us; but as we grew older we gradually substituted our judgment for theirs, always expanding our area of choice. When a politician tries to force his judgments on us, he is attempting to reverse the maturation process by shrinking our area of choice. And as our area of choice diminishes, so does the control of our lives and our confidence in our ability to deal with reality.

In pursuing our goals, we all act according to an "if-then" formula. For instance, *if* you are a student and want to become a painter, *then* you study painting. *If* you want to get to New York as quickly as possible, *then* you take a jet. *If* you want a high standard of living, *then* you try to find a job that pays well. We try to achieve our goals by using the means we deem most effective. Just as there are innumerable goals, so there are innumerable ways of achieving these goals. It is this infinite variety of means and ends that makes every person unique, according to the specific means and ends a person selects. To the extent that politicians meddle in our lives — to the extent that they tell us what goals to achieve or what means to employ — they are substituting their judgment for ours. And to the extent that our lives are planned according to a politician's specifications, our uniqueness as individuals is reduced, until we are eventually consigned to the anonymity of the anthill.

Human uniqueness and diversity make it more desirable to live in society than as a hermit on a desert island. Just to survive on a desert island would require your full time and energy. You would have to be a hunter, fisherman, carpenter, doctor, and more, just to stay alive. Living in a society allows you to benefit from the skills of other people — skills that represent uniqueness and diversity. The more diversity there is, the more you have to choose from, and the better chance you have of getting what you want. Thus we all benefit from diversity, and it is reasonable to encourage it as much as possible. But to introduce force into human relationships, to give one group of people — politicians — the power to tell another group how to live, is to destroy the foundation of human diversity. It is to shrink our range of alternatives to the confines of the politician's brain, which is small territory indeed.

There is another element of choice that is important here. Intelligent choices are those made with the most knowledge. The more you know about a situation, the more likely you are to make intelligent decisions about that situation. Consider the implications of this in your own life. Who knows the most about your life? Who knows the most about what your desires, goals, feelings and abilities are? You do, of course. Quite naturally, therefore, you are in a position to make the most intelligent and reasonable decisions concerning your own life. Only you possess the detailed information necessary to plan which actions are best for you. In every sphere where a politician presumes to make choices for you, then, the odds are overwhelming that his decisions will have worse consequences for you than your own would have. The politician is either deluded or lying when he claims to know better than you what is good for you. No one is in a better position to know what is good for you than you are. Another person cannot crawl into your skin to feel what you feel, and another person cannot decree, by force, what will make you happy. But this, in essence, is how politicians try to justify their existence.

Politicians coerce us to comply with their ideas of how we should live and behave. To coerce someone is to make him act against his will by force or the threat of force. The heavy hand of force is behind every political "solution." When the politicians promise a new playground, we will pay for it whether we want to or not. We will pay through our taxes or we will go to jail. If the zoning commissioner considers urban sprawl to be an esthetic menace, and if he thinks that the suburbs should remain "natural," then he uses force to keep people from building where he doesn't want them to. Political activity revolves around the principle of force, and force is anathema to choice. Where there is coercion, choice is lost.

Since choice is essential to human development, and since force nullifies choice, the use of force is anti-human. It is opposed to the vital elements of life and happiness. Any opportunity that expands our range of choice is good; any situation that restricts our range of choice is bad. If we are to regain control over our lives, politicians must give up some of their power. But it is unlikely that politicians will have an attack of ethical conscience and decide to loosen their paternalistic grip on us. It is possible, however, to strip politicians of their veil of legitimacy and to demon-

None of the Above ☑

strate that they do not represent the people they claim to represent. This can be accomplished by pushing for another alternative — "None of the Above is Acceptable" — on the voting ballots.

If enough people communicate to politicians that none of them are acceptable, that we don't want any of them to run our lives, then they may be forced, if they want to remain in office, to take a closer look at what people really want. Perhaps they will discover that the public is composed of responsible adults with individual desires, needs and goals. And perhaps the politicians will discover that the individuals themselves know best how to fulfill their desires, needs and goals, free from political interference. They may even discover that we value our uniqueness and diversity, and that we require freedom of choice to function to the full extent of our capabilities. Then, if we are lucky, some politicians may even assist us in regaining control over our lives so that we are free to choose for ourselves. This is the third alternative.

None of the Above ☑

Chapter 15

Order and Chaos

> "Great part of that order which reigns among mankind is not the effect of government. It has its origin in the principles of society and the natural constitution of men. It existed prior to government, and would exist if the formality of government was abolished. The mutual dependence and reciprocal interest which man has upon man, and all the parts of civilized community upon each other, create that great chain of connection which holds it together. The landholder, the farmer, the manufacturer, the merchants, the tradesman, and every occupation, prospers by the aid which each receives from the other, and from the whole. Common interest regulates their concerns and forms their law; and the laws which common usage ordains, have a greater influence than the laws of government. In fine, society performs for itself almost everything which is ascribed to government."
>
> Thomas Paine
> *Rights of Man, Part II*

It is commonly said that the main function of politicians is to bring order to society and that without politicians we would be faced with chaos and disaster. People who make this claim, however, are usually vague about what they mean by such terms of "order" and "chaos." Perhaps what

None of the Above ☑

is meant is that, without politicians, people would go around hurting each other. But people do this now *with* politicians, and they do it on a massive scale known as "war." The danger posed by the local bank robber is minor when compared to the threat posed by a massive military arsenal capable of immense destruction.

In any event, there is nothing especially disorderly about violence. In fact, much violence, especially in war, is highly ordered, in that it is carefully planned and engineered. Likewise, a bank robber usually plans his moves quite carefully before taking action. Such acts of violence have more "order" to them than the majority of our everyday nonviolent activities.

If, then, we equate order with planning, there is no intrinsic virtue in orderliness. Evil as well as good deeds can be carefully planned in advance. The important issue, of course, is not whether actions are planned, but what they are planned for. What is the *purpose* of a planned activity? Our moral view of the action will depend on this purpose.

It is true that politicians are engaged in planning of some kind, but this is not necessarily a mark in their favor. Every person, as we have seen, must plan to some degree, and these plans can be good or bad. The question we must ask about politicians is: What kind of planning are they engaged in? When looked at this way, we see that politicians concern themselves with planning the lives of other people. They devise plans of how others should live and they impose those plans by force. So it is misleading to say that politicians bring order to our lives. What they do, to be precise, is force their conception of order upon other people. "Order," in this case, turns out to be whatever the politician wants it to be.

Let's take a closer look at the term "order," since it tends to be a very slippery word. In actuality, "order" is an interpretation placed on a situation by a human mind. There is no "order" existing independently in nature. Facts are neither orderly nor disorderly; they are simply facts. When we view these facts, however, we evaluate them from a given frame of reference. If the facts fit into my pattern of thinking, I call them orderly. If they conflict with my way of thinking, I see them as disorderly.

Because I recognize the crucial role of individual choice and action, I can look at people milling about in a crowded department store and see marvelous order. A political mentality, on the other hand, might look at that same crowded store and be appalled by what it interprets as confused disorder. When I look at the store, I see people acting to fulfill their own desires and goals in a manner that is harmonious with their fellow humans.

None of the Above ☑

This, for me, is the epitome of order. When the political mentality views the same store, however, it is upset because all it can see is random, unconnected activity. The people in the store are not following a master plan — more specifically, they are not following *his* master plan — so his mind interprets the situation as disorderly.

This example illustrates how the judgment of orderliness will vary according to your point of view. If you place a high value on human autonomy and freedom of choice, then any situation where that autonomy and freedom of choice are realized will display, for you, a high degree of order. But if you value conformity and obedience, then you will have a militaristic conception of order, where there is order only when people are following orders in the literal sense.

The militaristic conception of order is that held by most politicians. They see order in regimentation, bureaucratic mazes and miles of red tape. If something is done with official approval, especially if it is accompanied by impressive-looking documents, then it is orderly. Or if a decision is made "democratically" by taking a vote, then the decision is orderly. But if a lone individual attempts an action on his own, the action is suspected of being "chaotic" and unplanned. All this really means, of course, is that the lone individual acts on the basis of his own plans instead of obeying the politician. This the politician finds inexcusable, so he condemns it as chaotic.

The political mentality, singularly unable to appreciate the importance of free choice in human affairs, invariably views the price mechanism of a free market, where price varies according to the fluctuation in supply and demand, as unplanned, chaotic or even anarchistic. We cannot be at the mercy of unplanned prices, he tells us, so we must call on government to regulate them. What the political mentality fails to see is that prices in a free market are not at all chaotic; they depend on the combined decisions and actions of millions of consumers and suppliers. It is true that prices are not planned in advance by a central computer; they are the consequence of many individual plans of action. But the political mentality does not see this. All he knows is that in a free market no one person or group plans what the price for a dozen eggs will be; so he interprets the situation as unplanned and hence disorderly. If the government forcibly imposes a price, however, the political mentality is satisfied, for now a tangible, concrete plan is being implemented.

It should be clear that the only confusion and disorder here is the thinking process of the political mentality. He cannot distinguish between order and decree. If a politician does not issue a proclamation, there is not order. If the politician does

None of the Above ☑

not force others to go along with his plans, there is anarchistic chaos. This is unmitigated nonsense. As long as people plan their own lives, and as long as their plans do not forcibly interfere with the plans of other people, there is order. The political mentality may not like what people, when they are free to choose, decide to do, but that is his problem, not theirs.

In the final analysis, the greatest impediment to human order is physical force. Force necessarily creates conflict. If everybody agreed to do something, one party would not resort to the use of force against another. When someone forces you to do something, therefore, a conflict exists between what you want to do and what he wants you to do. This conflict, perpetuated by more and more force, renders peaceful cooperation and competition impossible. The only order possible in such a situation is coercive regimentation and conformity. This is the order found in a slave camp.

Peaceful order, on the contrary, is order generated by people themselves rather than imposed on them by someone else. Voluntary cooperation is indispensable for this kind of order, and this kind of order is essential to human progress and happiness. This is the order that is the antithesis of political activity.

Chapter 16

Political Conflict of Interest

Politicians these days are falling all over themselves to prove they are clean and uncorruptible. The sight, silly to behold, has one candidate leading an "election reform" movement which would curtail the amount of private contributions to politics, another candidate staging an exhibitionist competition to reveal every penny of personal income, and yet another candidate trying to limit meals shared by lobbyists and office holders to "a hamburger and two cokes" (as if overeating is a cause of corruption). Perhaps the most popular method is to cite how corrupt one's opponents are, in an effort to make oneself look "clean" by comparison.

The futility of such measures should be readily apparent to anyone with common sense. As the saying goes, "the lady doth protest too much."

Notwithstanding this reform legislation, politicians will still wreak havoc on the lives of citizens. They are not about to curb their insatiable appetite for taxpayers' money, nor will they voluntarily cut off their other sources of power. Even

None of the Above ☑

if it is easy to see how foolhardy is the reform passion, however, there is one key phrase that cries for closer examination: *"conflict of interest."*

"Conflict of interest" — that phrase is operative in every new story of political corruption. But what is conflict of interest? We seem to have conflicting standards as to what exactly constitutes a conflict of interest.

A conflict of interest seems to be a conflict of pledges; pledges made by a politician to act in a given way after he assumes the office he sought in his campaign. Commonly we imagine that the important pledge is for the office holder to serve the whole of his constituency; that pledge is held to be sacrosanct. The other pledge, the conflicting one, is the promise he made to party members, supporters and/or financiers. It is this partisan pledge, although probably a tacit one, which seems to be the stronger of the two, the fulfilling of it more compelling. This makes sense. If the politician seeks another term or a higher office, it is his own people that he had better not cross. Loyalty to the voters is a nice sentiment, and a few politicians may even indulge in it occasionally, but politicians have made it clear time and again that nothing takes precedence over the interest of their party.

None of the Above ☑

Given a piece of legislation, the office holder is supposed to vote according to the best interest of his constituents. Yet every voter knows this is rarely the case. Foremost in the politician's mind is his party and its supporters. And here political rhetoric comes to the rescue. It just so happens, the politician assures us, that what is best for his party is also best for the country — and we are once again led down the primrose path of political chicanery.

There has been corrective legislation aimed at political financiers. If the proposed legislation in any way affects the office holder's financial ties, he is supposed to abstain, or he is supposed to divest himself of investments and business associations. This is especially true of judges, but theoretically it pertains to all politicians.

While the system is by no means perfect, so the argument runs, it does provide a means of ferreting out significant corruption. And, indeed, a good many politicians have been convicted on a conflict-of-interest rap. We have their political enemies to thank for that. Still, while we have gone after the financial conflicts, we have not cleansed the situation with regard to supporters.

What is called for is a new conflict of interest rule, this one to break the perfidious ties between a politician — and his own party!

None of the Above ☑

This idea may seem shocking at first. We take it for granted that a politician pays off in jobs and political favors to those who supported him during his campaign. Indeed, promises of special favors are an integral part of campaigning itself. But the politician claims to represent all of his constituents, and it is time to insist that he make good his claim by divesting himself of all interest conflicts.

This is certainly a reasonable request during these days of heated efforts to reform politics. Here is how it would work. Anyone accepting an elective office should be required to sever all association with his or her political party. In the same way that businessmen are required to divest themselves of investments and business associations when taking public office, so politicians accepting such posts should not be allowed to retain political involvement.

To have a senator or congressman or governor referred to as a "Democrat" or "Republican" should not be a meaningful designation when he is in the office supposedly representing "all the people." The excuse that party lines are a secondary consideration is wholly inadequate; a "party line" should be nonexistent for an office holder. There is no political district in this country in which all the voters are members of the very same party. Representatives of those districts inevitably catch themselves in dilemmas because serving constituents militates against unswerving party loyalty. A politician interested in more than one term in office knows he cannot alienate his party and its supporters. And a politician interested in only one term is unheard of.

When all is said and done, when the handshaking, baby kissing, flag waving and smiling for the cameras is finished, it usually winds up with "see what the boys in the back room want." And how could it be otherwise? Politics is big business with enormous sums of money involved, and voting is little more than a formality. If partisan political ties were severed, then those accepting political office would have only one cause to serve — the representation of the American people — not the self-serving ends of any political party.

None of the Above ☑

Chapter 17

Performance Bonding Of Politicians; Campaign Promise Insurance

Throughout American history, unfulfilled campaign promises have provided an inexhaustible source for political humor. Upon closer examination, however, there is little humor in broken campaign promises; on the contrary, they make a joke out of democracy and the vote.

The effects of such political deceit range from irritating to catastrophic. Broken political promises can lower our living standard or, in the case of broken anti-war promises, threaten our very survival. In short, individual American citizens must pay the price for policies they never wanted — indeed, for policies they hoped to prevent through their votes.

Through two centuries Americans have witnessed countless increments of "milestone" legislation designed to clean up politics. Yet politics remains soiled; corruption never wisps away as the reform legislation intends. A major reason for the failure to cleanse politics is quite simple:

None of the Above ☑

Politicians are still allowed, and even expected, to break campaign promises.

Politicians have become confidence men, promising everything and delivering whatever is convenient for them to deliver — which usually bears little resemblance to what their constituents want or need. To allow this to continue is to legitimate a fraud and an injustice. You may as well pick a candidate for his smile, or the way he combs his hair, for all the relevance his promises will have to his actions after he takes office.

Why not institute a new political practice which would be the essence of true reform? The idea, long overdue and much hungered-for in these times of the "credibility gap," is *performance bonding of politicians.*

It has long been common practice in private business to require the bonding of people in responsible positions. Why cannot this respected and time-proven business practice now be applied to politicians?

This suggestion, some may feel, questions the integrity of those in office. But this isn't necessarily true, any more than the bonding of businessmen questions their integrity. Performance bonding is simply a means of ensuring that a person does what he promises to do — and surely it is not unreasonable to expect politicians to abide by this basic standard of human decency.

None of the Above ☑

There seems to be an implicit assumption that a person's integrity cannot be challenged once he or she is in office. But this is obviously absurd in the face of overwhelming evidence to the contrary — the endless string of broken campaign promises and the blatant disregard for personal responsibilities by politicians. We are bombarded daily with news of Watergates and mini-Watergates. We witness politicians brazenly reversing themselves on issues when they deem it politically expedient, without so much as an acknowledgment of their broken promises. How many times have we heard a politician accuse the press or his opponents of "dirty politics" (is there any other kind?) if they expose his chameleon-like antics in disregarding his previous commitments? How long would a businessman remain bondable if he so irresponsibly disregarded his trusts?

Clearly, the voting citizenry requires a measure of protection from politicians. We need insurance to guarantee that what we vote for at the polls is what we get when the candidate takes office. If the politician breaks his word, he should assume responsibility for the damage that follows.

How could such a protection system work? First, all politicians would be required to buy a performance bond — a bond they must forfeit if they fail to deliver on their promises. The forfeited money would go to the public treasury, and

None of the Above ☑

from there to the individuals who were harmed the most by the politician's default. The higher and more responsible the office, the higher the bond would have to be.

Where would the money for the bond come from? The politician's party could put up the money, since it is the party that dangles him before us and assures us that he is a man of integrity. Instead of pouring millions of dollars into slick advertising campaigns, the political parties could vie with each other for the highest amount of performance insurance. The higher the bond, the more the voters would be assured of redress in the event of dishonesty and deceit.

The voters would evaluate the performance of the politician after his term expires, at the same time the forthcoming primary and general elections are held. If the voters decided that the politician acted responsibly, and tried to the best of his ability to fulfill his campaign promises, his bond would be returned in full, and he would gain the reputation of a good risk if he chose to run again for office.

If, on the other hand, the voters decided by majority vote (this is, after all, a democracy) that the politician ignored his promises and defaulted on his public trust, the bond would be forfeited. Not only would this compensate the victims of the politician's irresponsibility, but it would make

None of the Above ☑

subsequent bonding extremely difficult for the politician to obtain, making his return to politics unlikely. Thus we would have a kind of natural selection of politicians, with the dishonest weeded out and only the honest surviving.

Of course, the idea of performance bonding of politicians is not infallible, as we are all aware. We can't make a silk purse out of a sow's ear, so there will still be corruption and deceit in the political arena. Nevertheless, performance bonding of politicians is an attempt to patch an egregious hole in the American electoral system, perhaps the source most responsible for the mood of political corruption: the likelihood that voters will not get what they've been promised. A politician should not feel he can hoodwink the public and get away with it.

This plan would also inject a dose of realism into American politics. Politicians commonly promise a chicken in every pot and an answer to all problems, including poverty, unemployment, inflation and racial discrimination. The list is endless, and the politician looks more and more like the patent medicine peddler of fifty years ago, who sold a brew to cure "all that ails you."

But there is no quick cure for our problems unless it is fewer politicians, and there is no way that politicians can deliver on their extravagant promises. Performance bonding would make them

None of the Above ☑

think twice before making outlandish claims. And if politicians would spend less time making promises and more time investigating the disastrous effects of political meddling, they might even begin to question their own usefulness.

Performance bonding is a chance for the voting process to redeem itself to some degree. Imagine how nice it would be in an election to know that the candidates are directly answerable to you. And think what a pleasure it would be to be spared the insulting fairy tales, spiced with unfulfillable political promises, that our politicians spew forth year after year.

None of the Above ☑

Chapter 18

Politicoholism: An Epidemic Of National Concern

Politicoholism — a crippling disease of the brain and emotional system — must now receive serious attention by the American public. It has proved to be the number one cause of wars, economic disaster, inflation, abusive taxation, insufficient housing, unemployment, hunger — and of course, the age-old plague of government boondoggles.

Politicoholism is the number one health hazard in the United States. In fact, the problem is so serious that we suggest all political posters carry the sentence: "Warning! Politics may be hazardous to your health."

The unique characteristic of this disease is that those afflicted with it do not experience pain, but all with whom they come in contact, or "seek to serve," suffer varying degrees of pain and discomfort. Every American is familiar with the red-tape headache, not to mention the nausea induced by broken campaign promises. And the chronic ulcers, caused by a large chunk of our earnings being lifted by politicians for their pet projects, have reached almost epidemic proportions.

Can Politicoholism be detected at an early stage? The early symptoms are subtle, but they can be spotted by the careful observer. Warning symptoms usually appear in persons whose behavior seems fairly normal, if at times a bit messianic. The disease can infect nearly anyone, but it seems to favor ex-actors and ex-actresses, or those persons with a strong desire to be on stage but who never made it in show business. Most victims of the disease have a healthy, photogenic family, which becomes extremely important when the later stage known as "running for office" sets in. When at parties, dormant Politicoholics are full of suggestions on how you should run your life. Undaunted by their total lack of knowledge in the relevant areas, these future Politicoholics are convinced they could — and should — run everything from General Motors to the corner drugstore.

Budding Politicoholics are frequently detected by their obsessive use of the maxim, "There ought to be a law." This is known technically as the "coercion reflex." When asked his opinion on a social or economic problem, the Politicoholic twitches from the coercion reflex and blurts out involuntarily, "There ought to be a law."

None of the Above ☑

As the disease progresses, the Politicoholic finds himself unable to speak in anything but generalities and clichés. Thus afflicted, he is increasingly unable to communicate with friends and family. He feels a mounting sense of alienation. He may consider going to a speech therapist; but, more often than not, he attempts to compensate for his speech problem by transforming it into a virtue. The Politicoholic begins to see himself as a gifted and extraordinary individual. As the disease reaches other areas of his brain, he begins to view himself as savior of mankind, and he experiences an irresistible urge to offer himself as the vessel of salvation for his community, city, state, nation, or — in the most advanced cases — the world.

In its intermediate stages, Politicoholism manifests itself erratically and in various degrees. The Politicoholic commonly suffers from the delusion that he has complete control over his actions. The political meetings, fund raisers, and cocktail parties, he tells himself, are only part-time, and he can quit whenever he wants to. He restricts his political conversations to friends and small groups of people. Only occasionally does he wear campaign buttons and he never pins them to his underwear. The moderate Politicoholic may even display signs of modesty. During political discussions, he manifests the "I don't want to be pushy, but when you get tired of talking in circles,

None of the Above ☑

I'll be happy to supply an answer" syndrome. Or he may sit quietly until someone turns to him and says, "Come on, Fred, tell us what you think." (In later stages of Politicoholism, as the disease festers, this becomes known as "Waiting to be Drafted" and "Responding to Public Demand.")

In short, we have at this point the typical "social Politicoholic." Some can keep the disease under control at this level; their life goes on pretty much as usual.

But then the warning signals of acute Politicoholism begin to surface. The "social Politicoholic" finds himself delivering grandiose speeches, even when no audience is present, and he spends hours in front of a mirror smiling and waving his arms. Then, inexplicably, he starts to shake hands with every passerby he meets, and he terrifies mothers everywhere by rushing up to them and kissing their babies. Now the disease is beyond control. Whenever in public, the Politicoholic takes off his jacket and tie, unbuttons his collar and rolls up his sleeves. These, along with his sincerity wrinkles and meaningful stares, add to his credibility while he mouths platitudes about "the general welfare," "the good of society," and "the future of our country."

Here the Politicoholic is beyond hope. His entire system is so infested with this noxious disease that even our sophisticated medical and psycho-

None of the Above ☑

logical techniques are of no avail. The Politicoholic will crave the vote and he will stop at nothing to get it. He will lie, cheat, steal, or even worse, to win that election. Facts will never stand in his way. He will save people from themselves even if he has to kill them to do it. Politicoholism begins to take its toll, and throughout the land is heard the cry "Who will save us from our saviors?"

The causes of Politicoholism are not completely known at present, though there are several theories. Some doctors maintain that Politicoholism is a genetic infirmity which is transmitted from generation to generation. Other specialists regard it as a mental illness caused by an early and prolonged exposure to civics teachers and sociologists, coupled with a profound lack of anything important to say. Still other experts see Politicoholism as a contagious disease, transmitted by an unknown virus during election campaigns. The carriers of this virus are thought to be the active, chronic Politicoholics — known in polite company by the euphemism of "Politicians." Proponents of the contagion theory usually recommend a total quarantine of active politicians in order to prevent further spreading of the disease.

Whatever its cause, Politicoholism is a deadly disease. Politicoholics have frequently been the targets of unjust scorn and ridicule, but now the

None of the Above ☑

time has come to change our thinking about these poor unfortunates. The Politicoholic is not a depraved or evil person; he is *sick*, and he needs our help. We should establish centers for the treatment of Politicoholism where the victims of this blight can receive proper care in a humanitarian setting. (Funds for these institutions could be raised through Jerry Lewis telethons.) Less severe Politicoholics will be assisted in kicking the habit: they will be denied their repeated injections of public adoration, recognition, and acceptance — those addicting drugs that contribute so heavily to the spread of this disease. If the Politicoholic can withstand the severe withdrawal symptoms that follow, he can return to society and seek honest work.

Acute Politicoholics, while they may be beyond medical treatment, should not be cruelly tossed aside by an unfeeling public. As obnoxious as they seem, they are still fellow human beings. Recent proposals to put acute Politicoholics out of their misery, as an act of mercy, must be rejected totally as subhuman. More plausible is the suggestion that lobotomies be performed on all acute Politicoholics. But there are serious technical problems with this approach. Neurosurgeons warn that to perform brain surgery on a Politicoholic would require working within an inordinately small area, which would probably result in a large

None of the Above ☑

percentage of failures. Such failures, deprived of their last humanlike quality, would differ little from jackasses and hyenas. (Those who argue that even this would be a decided improvement are, of course, insensitive to the seriousness of this problem.)

There seems to be but one remedy for acute Politicoholics. They should be placed in a comfortable institution, beyond the reach of dangerous weapons, where they can act out their fantasies with each other, unencumbered by the real world. They can make speeches, solicit the votes of other inmates, plan the lives of one another, levy taxes in play money, issue decrees, and start imaginary wars for the good of their institution. Clearly, this is the only humanitarian solution to the problem of acute Politicoholism.

While feeling sympathy for these acute cases, however, let us not forget what is at stake. The acute Politicoholic, while himself an unfortunate victim, is extremely dangerous to others. The compassion we feel for him, therefore, should not overshadow our first priority: to get the Politicoholic off the street.

None of the Above ☑

Chapter 19

The Politician Is Best Who Works Least

"The ancient magistrates of this city correspond with those of the present time no less in form, magnitude, and intellect, than in prerogative and privilege. The burgomasters, like our aldermen, were generally chosen by weight — and not only the weight of the body, but likewise the weight of the head. It is a maxim practically observed in all honest, plain-thinking, regular cities, that an alderman should be fat...

"Thus, we see that a lean, spare, diminutive body is generally accompanied by a petulant, restless, meddling mind... Whereas your round, sleek, fat, unwieldy periphery is ever attended by a mind like itself, tranquil, torpid, and at ease; and we may always observe that your well-fed, robustious burghers are in general very tenacious of their ease and comfort; being great enemies to noise, discord, and disturbance — and surely none are more likely to study the public tranquility than those who are so careful of their own...

"As a board of magistrates, formed on this model, think but very little, they are less likely to differ and wrangle about favorite opinions — and as they generally transact business upon a hearty dinner, they are naturally disposed to be lenient and indulgent in the administration of their duties.

None of the Above ☑

"...The aldermen are the best-fed men in the community; feasting lustily on the fat things of the land, and gorging so heartily oysters and turtles that in process of time they acquire the activity of the one, and the form, the waddle, and the green fat of the other. The consequence is... that their transactions are proverbial for unvarying monotony — and the profound laws which they enact in their dozing moments, amid the labors of digestion, are quietly suffered to remain as dead-letters, and never enforced, when awake.

"Thus, it happens that your true dull minds are generally preferred for public employ, and especially promoted to city honors; your keen intellects, like razors, being considered too sharp for common service."

Washington Irving
Knickerbocker's History of New York

Politicians, like death and taxes, are an annoying reality. A problem of growing concern is what to do with our well-meaning neighbors when, abandoning their worthwhile careers, they succumb to the heady wine of local political office. This problem cries for attention. Because ordinary people seem to lose their sanity after they take office, we must try to minimize the damage. The same man who can run his personal finances in the black and cut costs and raise efficiency in his own work, suddenly, upon taking office, acquires the knack of spending public funds in the red, lowering productivity and raising costs. Since it is unlikely that we will dissuade our friends from run-

None of the Above ☑

ning for the city council or some other office, we need a plan to ensure that Mr. City Council does as little damage as possible while in power.

One such plan is the "extended vacation term." This can be tried first on the City Council level, and if it proves efficient, expanded to include all levels of political office. The mechanics of the plan are simple. Each year in office is divided into eleven months of mandatory traveling time — an extended vacation — and one month of personal vacation time. A politician does not have to travel during his personal vacation; he may even spend it in his hometown provided he does nothing that remotely resembles political activity. During the eleven months of his official term, however, Mr. City Council must travel — he must never return to his own city. To instill the proper spirit, and to guarantee that the plan will be carried out, inaugurations will be held at the airport just a few minutes before the politician's plane is scheduled to leave. Then the jubilant crowd will wave goodbye to the departing office holder, whom they will not see for another eleven months at least. For the first time in history, voters will have good cause to celebrate at an inauguration.

This traveling plan has several advantages. For one thing, it will no longer be necessary to provide office space for the politician. This saves money on expensive redecorating every time we

None of the Above ☑

change office holders. In addition, if there is no comfortable office complete with secretary and appointment book, the likelihood of Mr. City Council trying to stick around and miss his flight is almost nil. And he will be less inclined to order reams of official forms and personalized inter-office memos if there is no place to put them except in his suitcases. Moreover, there is the side benefit of raising the quality of neighborhoods where political offices once stood — the drop in the theft rate alone would be tremendous — which would release valuable real estate for more worthwhile projects such as bowling alleys and parking lots.

So much for some of the benefits of the extended vacation plan; now on to the mechanics of how the plan would work.

We should not spare expenses on these extended vacation trips; every accommodation should be first class. And, of course, there would be the padded expense account, without which Mr. City Council would lose his sense of identity. We should not be overly concerned if we find mink coats listed here and there as necessary expenses. After all, this has been going on for years anyway, and considering the overall picture, it is not really that great an expense to absorb.

Not only would the trip include first class accommodations for the politician, but it would also cover expenses for his family, secretary, bodyguard and P.R. person. The staff, however, would get somewhat cheaper accommodations in order to preserve the politician's sense of superiority and importance.

It may seem that the cost of these vacations would be prohibitive, but this is not the case if we take into account the horrendous cost of politicians when they are allowed to stay at home and do their "job." Even if $100,000 were allotted to each City Council member, the average city would escape with around $1 million annually. This money would be wasted, certainly, but it represents only a fraction of what is currently wasted in the present system.

For instance, with City Council members on extended vacations, we would be spared the enormous expense of appointed committees, which invariably led to the "garbage-dump game." This is a favorite pastime of politicians. It consists of appointing a committee to investigate a harebrained scheme, buying computer time to correlate meaningless data, hiring a printer to publish the findings in impressive looking tomes, and then contracting with a disposal service to tote away bales of reports and memos when the plan is discovered to be untenable.

We could also eliminate the mysterious "galloping estimates" which always plague public

None of the Above ☑

service projects. This is when Mr. City Council assures us, at the onset of his pet project, that it will cost the taxpayers only X number of dollars. This sum is usually moderate. Then, after the project is underway, the estimate doubles or triples — it seems there were a few miscellaneous incidentals that Mr. City Council failed to take into account. Of course, it is argued at this stage that the project must continue nonetheless, since it would be a shame to lose the money already invested in it. Then, after another few months, the estimate doubles or triples again, making the final cost as much as 10 times the amount of the original figure. When the project is finally completed, usually no more than two years after the initial deadline, the money invested in it alone would pay for years of extended vacations for the entire City Council.

Where would the money come from to pay for these extended vacations? More than likely, if a community is assured that its politicians will be gone for the entire year, people will gladly contribute to the cause. We could organize mass charity drives to raise enough money so that Mr. City Council would not even think of returning home ahead of time.

It has been argued that our politicians be required to visit other countries where they cannot speak the language and that they should not be provided with translators. The reasoning behind this suggestion is sound. Politicians, wherever they may travel, are still politicians, and there is the ever-present danger of them meddling in other people's affairs. This danger is minimized, however, if the politician is unable to communicate with those around him. He will give orders that no one will understand; and by the time he learns the language to a significant degree, his vacation will have expired.

This may eventually lead to a foreign exchange program with the politicians of various countries shuffled back and forth to places where they cannot understand what is being said. Thus unable to tell others what to do, politicians could transform themselves into cultural emissaries, perhaps demonstrating how to cook favorite dishes such as stew or borscht, from their native land. Just becoming traveling cooks would raise the productivity of politicians by at least 100 percent. But even if we cannot persuade our vacationing politicians to become culinary diplomats, we would all benefit, financially and psychologically, from their absence and silence.

None of the Above ☑

Chapter 20

Unethical Employment: The Social And Personal Consequences Of the Profession Of Politics

> "Hung Fung was a Chinese philosopher of well nigh a hundred years old. The Emperor once said to him: 'Hung, ninety years of study and observation must have made you wise. Tell me, what is the great danger of Government?' 'Well,' quoth Hung, 'It's the rat in the statue.' — 'The rat in the statue?!' repeated the Emperor. 'What do you mean?'... 'Why,' reported Hung, 'you know we build statues to the memory of our ancestors. They are made of wood and are hollow and pointed. Now, if a rat gets into one, you can't smoke it out — it's the image of your father. You can't plunge it into the water — that would wash off the paint. So the rat is safe because the image is sacred.'"
>
> Wendell Phillips
> (from Rudolph Rocker,
> *Pioneers of American Freedom*, page 37)

Doing honest work for an honest dollar has long been an American tradition. It gives a person a sense of pride and accomplishment, a sense of contributing to the general welfare of humanity.

None of the Above ☑

Honest work keeps us firmly in contact with the realities of life and it gives us a practical bent of mind. The virtue of honest work, with all of its benefits, is open to anyone who cares to pursue it — and fortunately the majority have chosen just this path.

But there is an entire class who do not participate in honest work, and consequently fail to attain a sense of pride, accomplishment and firm contact with reality. This is a minority group, but it is not a racial minority (although its members are often said to be of a special breed), nor is it a religious minority. Rather, this minority, whose members come from all walks of life, is better described as an "ethical minority." These people have chosen a different way of life. Rather than produce and interact with other people voluntarily, this class prefers to sponge off of the work of honest wage earners, and it delights in forcing its desires on others. This class, of course, is composed of politicians and bureaucrats. These unfortunates, having turned away from such honorable professions as sales, medicine, plumbing and accounting, have opted instead to join the ranks of the pseudo-profession known as "public office." And as long as they remain in public office they are depriving themselves of the opportunity to do honest work.

None of the Above ☑

The tragedy in this is that people who become politicians are usually the very ones whose characters can least withstand the strain of political office. These are the people who are out of contact with reality and who have no idea of simple cause and effect. They do not understand, for example, that you cannot spend ten dollars if you only have five dollars. Nor have these people learned the simple virtues of honesty and self-restraint. How many times have you heard wild, extravagant campaign promises that are immediately forgotten on inauguration day? Seeing that they lack personal virtue, it is no wonder when these people fall prey to the temptation of power after they assume office. And given the nature of political office, it is easy to understand why the longer they remain in office, the more tenuous their grasp on reality becomes.

In what other profession can you be hired to do a job and keep that job even if you do not deliver? If a contractor is paid to build a house, he must build the house or return the money he collected. But a politician can make all kinds of promises to the public and not deliver on any of them — and he may even get elected for another term. Although the majority of people may not want him, all he has to do is muster a plurality, however small, to defeat other candidates. The politician can thus ride into office on a small percentage of those eligible to vote. With this illusion of support, which the politician balloons into a "mandate of the people," the politician's ability to distinguish between fact and fiction becomes more and more fuzzy.

Politicians also live in an economic wonderland. If, in the real world, you consistently spent more than you earned, while expecting your neighbors to bail you out and pay for your mistakes, you would soon be in for a rude awakening. But politicians go on blithely, year after year, doing just that under the banner of "deficit spending," and we are the ones who pay the penalty in the form of higher taxes.

Power is an unfortunate thing in the hands of anyone, especially those lacking in common sense. Power enables politicians to institute all manner of half-baked schemes that don't amount to anything but public nuisances. Not only are these crazy projects hard on the public, they are also psychologically harmful to the politician. Being able to put unworkable schemes into action gives the politician the feeling that reality is made of Silly Putty and that it may be molded as he sees fit. This view only contributes to the general unsuitability of our politicians for honest work.

Mounds of red tape are another unpleasant side effect of having the fuzzy-minded in power. Freed from the everyday realities of life, the politician

None of the Above ☑

issues edict upon edict, generating tons of paper and red tape that smother and choke anyone who tries to penetrate the bureaucratic haze. After you fill out endless forms in triplicate, the dedicated public servants often forget who you are and what you want, leading to the distinct suspicion that you are there to serve them and not vice versa.

This role reversal of employer and employee is especially irritating. In the real world there is usually no doubt as to who is hiring whom. But in the Silly Putty world of politics, this distinction is often blurred and reversed. Although politicians don't admit outright that we are working for their benefit, they imply it in their actions.

If we cannot eliminate politics altogether, we should at least institute safeguards so that the morally infirm do not flock to it as they do now, harming both themselves and others. We should require that only those who are gainfully employed can participate in public office. This would ensure that the politician has at least a minimal foothold in the real world. Further, it should be required that the politician remain honestly employed during his term in office so as not to succumb to the strain and temptation of politics. This would have the added benefit of making politics a pastime or hobby, rather than a full-time occupation, which would considerably decrease its harmful effects.

None of the Above ☑

Finally, we should set a time limit on how long a person can spend in the political arena. This would decrease the likelihood of the politician becoming permanently severed from the real world, which happens so frequently after prolonged exposure to high office.

Such measures, however, as desirable as they may be, are at best palliative. The only permanent solution is to find honest work for those now in public office, and to convince our "public servants" that they would be doing themselves and everyone else a favor if they joined the ranks of the honestly employed.

None of the Above ☑

Chapter 21

Between The Lights

I appeared on a television program with a representative from the League of Women Voters who wished to reply to my attack on politicians. I will, for the sake of this recounting, call this lady Ms. Jones.

Ms. Jones was an attractive, businesslike woman with a firm but pleasant manner. After listening to some of my caustic remarks about politics and politicians, she leaned forward in her chair and began intense cross-examination.

"Surely you would agree, Mr. Leon, that politicians, whatever their faults, serve a vital function in our society."

"What function do you have in mind?" I asked.

"I'll give you one obvious example," she replied. "Did you drive to the television studio this afternoon?"

"No," I said, "I walked."

"In that case, did you cross any intersections with street lights?"

"Yes, several, as a matter of fact," I said.

None of the Above ☑

Her eyes sparkled as she dangled the bait in front of me. "Am I correct," she asked, "in assuming that you obeyed the traffic signals?"

"Yes," I said, naively unaware that I had just taken the bait.

Ms. Jones smiled and set the hook. "So, Mr. Leon, even you admit the need for political regulations, and even you obey those regulations. The politicians made those laws and you obey them. It seems clear that, whatever you say in theory, you concede a function for politicians in practice."

I was apparently in a bind. Was I a "traffic anarchist," opposed to all regulations and traffic signals? Did I favor the merciless running down of pedestrians and the chaotic crashing of cars?

"It seems to me," I said, "that by obeying the traffic signals I was simply exercising a dose of common sense. Like most people, I have no desire to get run over by a truck. Whether the government put those lights there or someone else did doesn't make me feel any different; I *still* don't want to get run over by a truck. So I obeyed the traffic signals, not out of any respect for politicians, but out of respect for trucks."

Ms. Jones looked mildly annoyed. "Mr. Leon, whatever your motives may have been for obeying the traffic signals, you are still admitting that there is an important function served by the political mechanism."

None of the Above ☑

"No, not at all," I replied. "Let's be realistic about this. The government is monstrously huge. Do you really think, Ms. Jones, that we need so many politicians and bureaucrats to keep the traffic signals running? Maybe the fellow who runs the corner drugstore could switch on a nearby signal when he arrives for work in the morning, and then switch it off at night when he leaves. I mean, I hate to think that we suffer as we do at the hands of politicians for the sake of a few traffic lights. Surely there are some alternatives."

"Perhaps," Ms. Jones replied. "But even if that is the case, the politicians you dislike are responsible for the traffic signals as they presently exist."

"Really?" I asked. "I would be willing to bet that those signals were manufactured by private industry. I doubt if many politicians could construct a traffic signal."

My adversary paused for a moment, as if waiting for me to acknowledge that I wasn't serious. Then she patiently attempted to clarify her point. "Mr. Leon, I think you know what I mean. At the very least, politicians keep the signals running."

"Do you mean that our elected officials go out and personally repair traffic signals?"

"No, of course not." Mrs. Jones was losing some of her patience with me. "I think you're being obstinate, Mr. Leon. My point is simply that politicians are ultimately responsible for traffic signals and other public services. For example, they pay for these services so that we all may benefit from them."

"Now I'm really confused," I said. "Again, at the risk of sounding obstinate, I think it's quite clear that the taxpayers, not the politicians, pay for public services. So let me get this straight: politicians don't manufacture the traffic signals, they don't repair and maintain them, they don't plan or coordinate their placement, nor do they pay for them. Yet we are supposed to believe that without politicians we wouldn't have traffic signals and orderly traffic. That's a great job. Where else can you be so important and be paid so well for not doing all these things? By the same logic, I am responsible for commercial airlines. I don't know how to build, repair or run them, and don't pay for their manufacture. By political standards, my credentials are impeccable. I should be elected president of all the airlines."

Ms. Jones looked puzzled. "Do you mean to say," she asked, "that politicians have nothing whatever to do with traffic signals and other public services?" "Not at all," I said. "Their primary job is to decide how much money should be forced out of the taxpayers, and then to decide how they, the politicians, wish to spend that money. That's the peculiar thing, you see. Ordinarily, if a person goes around taking money from others by force and then spending that money, we don't say he has a "job" — we say instead that he is a thief — and we don't grant him our respect. Least of all do we say that he is an indispensable part of our welfare. Now my point is that a thief by any other name is still a thief even if he goes around building traffic lights."

"But I just don't understand this," Ms. Jones protested. "If the politicians didn't do their job, we would have chaos and disorder. Everything would be a mess."

"Let's examine this more closely," I suggested, "since we seem to have overlooked something. It's true that I obeyed some traffic signals when I walked to the studio this afternoon, but let's not forget the area *between* the lights. Most of the distance I traveled was not regulated by lights; by your standards, those vast stretches of sidewalk were in a virtual state of anarchy. There were no lights or laws telling me how to get from one place to another, to avoid bumping into other people and so on, yet I managed quite well. I didn't fall down once, or slip off any curbs, or run into any walls, and neither did any of the other people on those sidewalks. In short, by pursuing my own goals and acting on my own judgment without the alleged assistance of a politician, I was able to walk where I wanted to go, and to do so in harmony with my fellow human beings. Yet to hear you describe it, people are so feeble-minded they cannot get along without the meddling of politicians. But I disagree. People *are* able to plan their own lives and they don't need a politician to plan for them."

"But," asked Ms. Jones, "don't you agree that planning is necessary in at least some cases?"

"I never said I was against planning. On the contrary, planning is necessary in most areas of life. It's not an issue of planning or not planning. The issue is: *Who* does the planning? My opposition to political planning in no way implies chaos or disorder. I am against political planning because it forces people to act against their own judgment. I think each person should plan his or her own life. But the politician, in your view, should plan for other people whether they want it or not. It is likely, Ms. Jones, that many people watching this program want less interference in their lives. They are tired of being told what to do, how to do it, and when to do it, by someone who knows and cares nothing about them. People want to run their own lives. And if you and I are as aware of the problem as we like to think we are, then the best thing we can do is to leave people alone and respect their right to make their own decisions. So it's not a matter of whether there should be order in society, but whether that order should be generated from within by the voluntary activity of the individuals concerned, or whether that order should be imposed from without by the heavy hand of a politician."

"Now, Ms. Jones, if you want to hire a politician to plan your life for you, that's fine — I wouldn't presume to tell you how to live. But please, I implore you, restrict his beneficent efforts to your behalf and instruct him to leave me alone. I would consider that downright neighborly of you. When the politician offers his services to me, I just want a simple option: I want to be able to say, 'No, thank you.' And if, like an obnoxious salesman, he persists in annoying me, I want the right to say, 'Get Lost!' and to slam the door unceremoniously in his face."

None of the Above ☑

Chapter 22

Everything Works

"The World's Oldest Known Specification for STEELMAKING:

"In 1895, someone digging in the ruins of an armorer's workshop in Tyre, Syria, found sword blades in several stages of manufacture. He also discovered, rolled up in a copper tube, a parchment containing the following instructions in ancient Syrian characters:

"'Let the high dignitary furnish an Ethiop of fair frame and let him be bound down, shoulders upward, upon the block of the God Bal-hal, his arms fastened underneath with thongs, a strap of goatskin over his back, and wound twice round the block, his feet close together lashed to a dowel of wood, and his neck projecting over and beyond the end of the block.... Then let the master workman, having coldhammered the blade to a smooth and thin edge, thrust it into the fire of the cedarwood coals, in and out, the while reciting the prayer to the God Bal-hal, until the steel be of the color of red of the rising sun when he comes up over the desert toward the East, and then with a quick motion pass the same from the heel thereof to the point, six times through the most fleshly portion of the slave's back and thighs, when it shall have become the color of the purple of the king. Then, if with one swing, and one stroke of the right arm of the master workman it severs the head of the slave from his body,

None of the Above ☑

and display not nick nor crack along the edge, and the blade may be bent round about the body of the man and break not, it shall be accepted as a perfect weapon, sacred to the service of the God Bal-hal, and the owner thereof may thrust it into a scabbard of asses' skin, brazen with brass, and hung to a girdle of camel's wool dyed in the royal purple.'

"If you can consider this procedure strictly from the steelmaking standpoint, you'll notice that it covers the complete manufacture of a steel product, including cold-working to given tolerances, heat treatment for a specified time, a delayed quench to a specific color, quality control, and even packaging.

"Yet twentieth-century steel manufacturers reject this method for heat treatment and tempering of steel, no matter how valid it is from a purely metallurgical standpoint.

"I submit that to argue any moral issue pragmatically is to try to justify the right of a man to pursue this steelmaking process; in essence, to argue that one man owns the life of another."

— (from a *Rampart Journal* article by William J. Colson.)

[*Just as modern day steelmakers have improved upon the ancient Syrian process, future societies will replace the present political system — and for the same reasons.*]

There is a lot of concern nowadays that "nothing works," that the system is failing. Politicians fall over each other denying that they are part of this non-working system; they offer themselves instead as "non-establishment" or "non-political" politicians. (Of course, these same politicians have been around for years as cornerstones of the establishment, but let's overlook this for the moment.) This latest political shuffle seems to be a response to the growing public dissatisfaction with the consequences of how things are being run. The politicians have found their scapegoat in the "system," and they are ritualistically denouncing it and proposing ways to make it "work" better. This is nothing more than ritual because they have not really rejected the system at all, and their proposals to make it work better are just more of the same thing we have always had.

Political action still means spending more tax money and widening political control over private lives. Both of these tactics were the basis for the "old" system, and both are the basis of any allegedly new solutions that the politicians come up with. Contrary to what we are told, the old system did work and it is still working — it is just that more and more people object to the results.

The problem with the present system is not that it doesn't work but that it works too well. It accomplishes precisely what it was intended to accomplish. The political system in America today is quite efficient in controlling those within its grasp. Politicians may bicker over how tax money

None of the Above ☑

is to be spent, but they don't argue over whether there should be taxes at all. Or they may argue over whose grand, expensive scheme for a better society should be implemented, but they don't argue over whether any politicians' social plans should be implemented in the first place. All new political schemes are formulated within this context, which means they are not really "new" in any fundamental sense. Energetic politicians who promise to make the system "work" fail to realize that the system is working and has been for some time. Their innovative programs are nothing more than old wine in new bottles.

The question, then, is not whether the system works, but whether we like the *way* it works. Just because something works doesn't mean it is desirable. Concentration camps work, if your purpose is to enslave people. Stealing works, if all you care about is money. Lying works, if you don't give a damn about your personal integrity. Literally anything, no matter how monstrously immoral, will work, depending on your desires and how you define the term "work."

To say that the present political system works, therefore, is not to approve of it. On the contrary, since the purpose of the political apparatus is to limit our range of free choice, it is to our disadvantage that it works. We would be much better off if it didn't function at all.

None of the Above ☑

This brings us to the subject of "loopholes." Many public-spirited crusaders cry out incessantly against tax loopholes and loopholes of other varieties. It is not fair, they say, that some people can escape the legal penalties for minding their own business. These same crusaders complain about bribery in government which, they say, prevents the government from working properly.

Now it is quite true that loopholes and bribery prevent the government from functioning as efficiently as it might otherwise. But instead of complaining about these things, we should thank our lucky stars. It is a small consolation, perhaps, but it is comforting to know that as government increases in size it becomes less efficient and more open to corruption. If our government were as "efficient" as its virtually unlimited resources and manpower permitted it to be, the flicker of liberty remaining in this country would have long ago been extinguished.

In a system filled with self-contradictory and often unintelligible regulations, the only choices open to those who must survive within it are to subvert it or ignore it. Ignoring it is hardly possible, given the millions of "civil servants" who are dedicated to cataloging and ferreting out each productive citizen and seeing that a cut of his output goes to the government. That leaves subverting, or "corrupting," the system. The small

None of the Above ☑

businessman who bribes a building inspector because an incoherent maze of building codes makes it impossible for him to stay in business any other way, is just one among thousands who appreciate how "corruption" in a repressive system allows it to function. The worker who "cheats" on his income tax in an effort to hold the political thieves at bay is a grateful recipient of loopholes. It is only those loopholes which make it possible for the system to continue functioning; if a vampire doesn't leave you enough blood to survive, it will be without a source of its own survival.

In an age of omnivorous government where open defiance is easily quashed, loopholes and corruption provide a few of the rare opportunities for the individual to exercise his freedom of choice in relative safety.

We see, therefore, that how we evaluate the "efficiency" of a system, or whether that system "works," will depend entirely on what that system accomplishes. In a free society where the system is geared to preserving individual freedom, the better the system works, the more we will like it. And we will disapprove of loopholes because we will resent attempts to violate human freedom. But many people unthinkingly adopt this attitude toward whatever system they happen to be living under. This is "our" country, we are patriotic Americans, so we must want the system to work.

None of the Above ☑

But the "system" in this case is no more ours than it is American. We did not invent it and it is not indigenous to America. Rather, the political way of doing things has been with mankind ever since one group of men got it in their minds to tell another group what to do. The outward appearance of the political process has changed, of course, depending on the time and country. But the basic mechanism remains unchanged.

If anything represents the American spirit and attitude, it is hostility to being pushed around. In view of this, nothing could be more American and more in the spirit of the Boston Tea Party, than to resist politicians by whatever means we have at our disposal. And if those means include being alert to loopholes, then let us, in the name of patriotism, take full advantage of them.

None of the Above ☑

Chapter 23

To Go Forward, Put Your Mind In Gear

Politics is an intellectual anesthetic. It can dull the mind, put it to sleep, or even kill it permanently. This is not an incidental side effect; it is a calculated result that keeps the politician in business. What did you feel the last time you watched a political convention on television for any length of time? If there is one thing you felt, it was bored. And if there is one thing you didn't feel, it was intellectually stimulated. Intellectually active people do not think in a rut; they consider new ways, new alternatives; many of which may never have been attempted before. But this kind of questioning and independence spells death for politics. Politicians must convince you that the alternatives they offer you — for example, between the Democrats and Republicans — are the only alternatives that exist. But politicians are as trustworthy here as they are in fulfilling their campaign promises. You can bet on it: if a politician says something, it is probably false. This al-

None of the Above ☑

most provides a standard for measurement of truth and falsehood.

Considering alternatives; the willingness to challenge and explore — this is what freedom and independence are all about. Trusting yourself to discover workable solutions to problems — this is the biggest personal contribution you can make to the demise of political meddling. *What* you think isn't nearly as important as the fact *that* you think. You may come up with an idea today only to replace it with a better idea tomorrow. That's fine; the specifics will change, evolve and improve. But keeping your mind active, always challenging and questioning — that is the important thing.

Considering alternatives is, of course, what this book is all about. We have suggested that human problems can be solved through nonpolitical means — that is, without the use of force and fraud. This will seem strange to many people because we have been inundated since childhood with the idea that the political way is the way to get things done. But that simply isn't so. *You* are best able to deal with *your* problems in your own way.

Let's consider a few alternative ways of doing things. These are suggestions and intermediate steps, not final solutions. They are offered in the hope of stimulating your thinking so that you can

None of the Above ☑

improve upon them and devise new alternatives of your own.

Has it ever occurred to you, in view of modern technology, how utterly primitive is our present method of voting? People must leave their homes, wait in long lines and use relatively crude voting machines. You can talk to a person on the other side of the world in the comfort of your own home, but you cannot vote — a much less complicated process — in the same way.

This leads to an alternative suggestion. Why not hook in the voting process to telephone lines, where, with a special attachment, you could indicate your preference by phone, which would then be tabulated by computer? Certainly this is within the scope of current technology and would eliminate much of the mess that now hampers the voting process. This would have an extra advantage if a "None of the Above" option were available. The disgruntled voter who doesn't want to waste an hour or so at the polls merely to express his disgust with politicians can now vent his anger in the comfort and privacy of his own home. No longer must he inconvenience himself to tell politicians that he doesn't like what they are doing.

Let's consider another subject: political representation. Elected politicians, we are told, represent us. But this is nonsense, as any sane person can see. Where is the politician that represents

None of the Above ☑

you? Where is the politician that consults you and acts as you wish him to? Where is the politician that you can fire, or refuse to pay, if he does not render satisfactory service? Representation in the present system is a sham; it is nothing more than a front for political power.

In actual fact, the idea of one person "representing" a group of persons is impossible when that person will be required to make decisions that have not been fully agreed upon beforehand. If 10 people decide they are in favor of X, they may appoint a representative to vote for X in their behalf. This is representation. But to give this representative a blank check on future choices that have not yet been decided by unanimous consent of the group — to say that this one person speaks for the group when he has not even consulted the group on a specific issue — is nonsense of the worst kind.

If representation cannot truly be achieved, it can at least be improved upon. This brings us to another alternative. Instead of the present system where you are forced to pay for a "representative" whom you may despise with a passion, we could institute a system whereby a representative could sell his services on the market. Here is basically how it would work.

A person who wished to be a representative would advertise his credentials, background and

None of the Above ☑

so forth. This would take the place of political campaigns. Then, instead of voting, people would simply subscribe to the representative of their choice. This would be done by paying a fee of, say, two dollars per year. A representative who appealed to a fair number of people would thus be paid quite well for his services, but he would continue to be paid only as long as he kept his customers happy. If he displeased them, as with any other service, they would shop elsewhere.

In order to gain a seat in the national congress, a representative would have to have a stipulated number of clients (for example, 500,000). The number of clients required for state and local representation, of course, would be considerably less. In any case, he would represent only those clients who pay his salary and he could not presume to represent anyone else. This alone would eliminate recourse to the "mandate of the people" ruse so often used by politicians.

In addition, this plan would encourage price competition. One representative might offer the same service as another representative but for less money. People could then compare prices and shop for economy, or not at all — actions totally impossible under the present system. And remember, this plan would not require taxation to pay the salary of representatives. They would be paid

None of the Above ☑

for voluntarily, according to their fee and number of clients.

These suggestions and others like them are quite simple and straightforward, yet they open up new vistas that are usually ignored. Just allowing your mind to wander and to investigate new ideas at random will frequently pave the way toward solving problems that once seemed hopelessly complex. As stated before, these ideas are only suggestions, not final answers. But in attempting to combat the political plague, any step in the right direction, however small, is to be applauded.

None of the Above ☑

Chapter 24

Gadfly At The Post Office

Virtually no one would disagree with the view that bureaucracy invariably leads to inefficiency. And when this inefficiency is insulated from the world by the protective cover of a government monopoly, the results are ever greater costs and diminishing services.

We've all watched the constant growth of government agencies and the entangled mess called "the system." As it strives to increase efficiency, provide more services and reduce costs, the results are just the opposite — less efficiency, poor service and higher costs. Every aspiring candidate promises the former and, after elected, delivers the latter.

Meanwhile, the poor, beleaguered public has had to survive in spite of bureaucratic "services," and we've come to view them, along with death and taxes, as inevitable.

We've all had personal experiences upon direct confrontation with "the system." Although many have suffered grievously from these encounters, sometimes there are entertaining aspects — my

None of the Above ☑

attempt to obtain a passport being one such episode.

This was my second trip to the post office to apply for a passport. On my first trip, I had brought a small snapshot of myself which, although it was the proper size, had a glossy finish. This, I was promptly informed, was unacceptable. So here I was again, non-glossy photo firmly in hand, struggling to keep my good humor during my twenty-minute wait in line.

Finally it was my turn and I approached the window. I was greeted by a pleasant appearing fellow wearing glasses. He glanced impatiently at the clock. "Well," he said, "it's five minutes past three and this window is supposed to close at three, but I'll go ahead and take care of you."

"It's a good thing you're doing this," I replied, "because I wouldn't want you to miss the opportunity."

"Opportunity? What opportunity?"

"To meet me and take care of me. If I had left, you would have missed that. But now we both benefit. Isn't that great?"

The clerk obviously didn't think it was too great, but he nodded his head. I handed him my birth certificate, photograph and application. He studied the birth certificate closely, muttered something about the date, and then called over his

None of the Above ☑

coworker — the same woman who originally rejected my glossy photo.

"Is this the correct date of your birth?" she asked.

"Yes, that's correct."

"Well, there is a problem here. This certificate was signed three years later."

"So?" I replied innocently, failing to appreciate the extreme gravity of the situation.

"That makes it a deferred birth certificate."

"That can't be," I said.

"Why not?"

"Because I was a premature baby."

They looked at me sharply. They didn't understand what I meant, and frankly, neither did I, but it seemed appropriate.

"We can't accept this," the woman said. "If this signature belongs to the doctor who delivered you, then it's all right, but we don't know if this is the doctor's signature or not. Do you remember the doctor's name?"

"No, I'm sorry. It was fifty-three years ago. But the next time around I'll be sure to catch his name or maybe even get his business card."

After a few more minutes of equally productive conversation, we reached a compromise. They would send the certificate to the passport office and leave the decision to them. This was at least reassuring. Since this certificate was the only one

None of the Above ☑

I had, it was good to know that there was still hope that the government would not declare me to be nonexistent.

Then the male clerk began to examine my passport application. When he reached the back of the form, he protested. "You didn't answer all of the questions."

"Oh, which ones did I forget?"

"This one that asks when you are making your trip."

"I left that blank," I explained, "because I don't have definite plans as yet."

"But we have to know when you are making your trip."

I repeated myself. "I'm not planning to make a trip. I just want to have a passport in case I do decide to travel."

The clerk wouldn't budge an inch. "If you don't put a date down, you can't get a passport. That's the rule."

"But if I have no plans, how can I put a date down?"

The clerk was becoming visibly irritated. "I don't know anything about that. All I know is that they want this form completely filled out, and unless you list a date you won't get a passport."

"I see. So you want a date?"

"Yes."

"Does it matter when the date is?"

None of the Above ☑

"No," he replied. "It just has to be a date." With that the clerk slid the application across to me and signaled me to fill in the space.

I nodded my head, wrote down June 7, 1984 and slid the form back.

The clerk did a double-take. "1984! That's ridiculous!"

I was apparently too frivolous with such serious business. "You said any date was fine. If you don't like it, change it. Put down any date you like."

"No, it's up to you. But there's another question you left blank. How long do you plan to be gone?"

I was puzzled. "Do you mean how long will I be gone on a trip I am not planning to take?"

"Yes."

"I don't know. If I'm not planning the trip, how do I know how long I won't be there?"

"All I know is that you have to fill in the blank."

"Well, how about a month or two?" I suggested.

"You have to be more specific."

"How about a month?"

"A month is good," the clerk replied.

So I put down one month for the trip I was not going to take in 1984. But it wasn't over yet.

None of the Above ☑

"When are you planning your next trip?" the clerk inquired, with a straight face.

"Do you mean when am I planning a trip after the one I am not going to take in 1984?"

"That's right."

"Well, that could be almost anytime."

"But I need a specific time."

"Okay," I said. "How about a year later?"

"Whatever you like. Now there is one more thing. What country are you going to be visiting?"

"What country will I not be going to on the one-month trip I am not going to take in 1984?"

"Yes."

"Europe?"

"You must be more specific. I need a country."

"How about France? That sounds like a nice place not to visit for a month in 1984."

"France is good," the clerk said. He appeared to be satisfied, and I seemed to be nearing the end of my ordeal. Then he pointed to an oath at the end of the form. I was to "solemnly swear" that the information I provided was correct, and some unpleasant penalties were threatened for falsifying information.

"Wait a minute!" I protested. "Now I have to swear that all the lies I told are true. This is ridiculous."

"All I know is that you have to sign the pledge if you want the passport."

None of the Above ☑

"All right," I said, taking my life in my hands, "I'll sign."

Two days later I received the passport. Somebody must have done something right.

None of the Above ☑

Chapter 25

Optimism or Pessimism?

The ideas in this book may strike some readers as pessimistic or even destructive. Why am I so critical of politicians? Isn't there anything good that can be said about them? What would I put in the place of politicians?

First, the ideas in this book are not destructive in the least. True, I would like to see politicians out of work, but this is no more destructive than if you hired someone to rid your house of mice. As to what I would put in the place of politicians, the answer is nothing, hopefully — in the same way that you would not replace the mice in your house with some other rodent.

What do I have against politicians? Simply the fact that they are politicians? Isn't there anything good that can be said about them? Perhaps, on a personal basis. Some politicians are undoubtedly interesting and compassionate human beings, and they probably have other valuable qualities as well. These are the qualities that would interest me if I were their friend. But politicians are not out to befriend me because this would require my

None of the Above ☑

consent and cooperation. Politicians leave me no choice; they impinge on my right to choose freely and to associate with whom I please. So their individual qualities do not interest me because they do not employ these qualities in relating to me. Instead, they use their position of power to impose their desires on me as to how they want me to live. Whether a politician is friendly or charming or witty is, therefore, of no interest to me because there is no difference between being pushed around by a friendly politician and being pushed around by an unfriendly politician. When you rid your house of mice, you do not bother to distinguish the mice with good personalities from the mice with bad personalities. All of them are pests as far as you are concerned.

If the politician wants to be regarded as just ordinary folk, and if he wants to be judged according to his personal character (as we judge ordinary people), then he should relinquish his stranglehold on his neighbors and leave them alone. After all, an ordinary person does not shove his neighbors around, telling them what they may and may not do; he leaves them a choice as to whether they want to associate with him. This is where his personal qualities become important. The more his neighbors admire his character and personality, the more they will want to associate with him, either personally or professionally. But not so the politician. Whether we judge him virtuous or vicious, we will be forced to follow his dictates. So why should we care whether a politician is a nice guy or not? He will meddle in our lives regardless of our opinion of him.

But are not many politicians at least well-intentioned, and do not they deserve our respect for this? To answer this, we must find out what "well-intentioned" means. If it means that many politicians are doing what they think is right, that's fine, but it is hardly news. Where on this earth is a person who does not do what he thinks is right? The most tyrannical dictator probably does what he thinks is right — for himself.

Now doing what you think is right is both necessary and desirable. But if politicians are to be praised for this, why don't they extend the same courtesy to other people? Why won't the politicians let us do what we think is right? Why must they constantly interfere in our lives? If "well-intentioned" means doing what you think is right, basic decency requires that you permit other people to be well-intentioned also; that you permit them to do what they think is right.

The trouble with politicians is not that they do what they think is right but that they force others to do what they, the politicians, think is right. Some politicians may have good intentions but this doesn't change the facts; and it doesn't merit

None of the Above ☑

our praise any more than good intentions by Hitler or Stalin would change our estimation of them. If doing what you think is right is such a virtue, then we should have as much of it as possible. This means a free society where politicians are conspicuously absent.

What of the charge that I am pessimistic? This is far from true. If anything, I am optimistic — I am confident in the ability of people to manage their own lives free from political interference. The political mentality, on the other hand, is truly pessimistic. It sees humans as so feeble and corrupt that they require the iron-fisted guidance of politicians. If this is true, the question naturally arises: If humans are inherently feeble and corrupt, how can we trust politicians to guide us since as humans they are feeble and corrupt as well? This question, of course, is unanswerable.

Am I overly optimistic? Do I have an unrealistically high estimation of human nature? Not at all. As creatures of choice, humans have the capacity for good or evil, and many have unfortunately chosen to wreak havoc on their fellow humans. The very existence of politics testifies to this destructive ability.

It is precisely because of man's capacity for evil that we need to protect ourselves as much as possible from those who decide to inflict harm. This is why politicians are such a threat. They control vast and complex machines of organized violence. They have at their disposal efficient means to impose their wishes on others. The more we can dismantle this coercive apparatus, the better chance we have of diminishing and isolating the effects of evil men. As things stand now, however, a handful of power seekers can make its will felt over an immense area. In a free society there would still be evil men, but they would lack this convenient avenue for carrying out their deeds. If we cannot eradicate the desire of some to rule others, we can at least minimize to the greatest extent possible the organized system by which this desire to rule can be implemented.

I am frequently asked the following question: "If you don't like the present system, then why don't you try to change it instead of griping about it? Why don't you run for office yourself or support a candidate who shares your views, instead of doing nothing?"

It is interesting how some people interpret a rejection of political activity as doing nothing. What this really means is that if you attempt to persuade others to accept your point of view voluntarily, you are "doing nothing." "Doing something" for the political mentality is equivalent to doing something politically — that is, doing something by force.

None of the Above ☑

Why not support a candidate who shares my views? Because if a person shared my views he could not be a candidate. You may as well tell a civil rights advocate to join the Ku Klux Klan. An anti-political politician is not to be trusted since the best way to be against something is simply not to participate in it.

Why can't the system be changed from within? Why not enter the political arena with the expressed intent of changing it? Simply because good intentions are not enough. You can be chock full of good intentions but you will not stop an avalanche by standing in its way. The avalanche will continue on its path, taking you along with it. The best you can do is to get out of its way and to advise others to do the same while hoping that eventually it will lose momentum.

Just as the way to lessen crime is not to join the ranks of the criminals, so the way to lessen the harmful effects of politicians is not to swell their ranks by joining with them. There may be more glory and fame in running for political office, as contrasted with spreading one's ideas nonpolitically, but it is not glory and fame that those concerned with human freedom are after. Running for political office may garner more publicity, but what kind of publicity? The public does, and should, look with a jaundiced eye upon any self-proclaimed anti-politician who uses political candidacy as a means of attracting attention.

Walking contradictions are not to be trusted — especially when they are asking for power.

None of the Above ☑

Chapter 26

How To Achieve And Maintain Your Freedom Through Political Actions And Other Forms Of Violence

Introduction

Thus far we have criticized and poked fun at politics and politicians. The material is admittedly lopsided, presenting only the bad side of politics. Out of fairness, therefore, it is only fitting that we devote a chapter to the opposition. We solicited a leading political theorist to write a powerful defense of political action, and we are honored to present his conclusions in this, the final chapter of our book. Before we get to this remarkable chapter, however, a few introductory comments are in order.

For thousands of years, man has attempted to influence the thoughts and actions of his neighbors by devising political mechanisms that will guide us all to a condition of universal peace in a world of bountiful supply amid unalloyed pleasures.

None of the Above ☑

The academy has spewed forth scholars at an ever-increasing rate, each armed with his own bit of intellectual chamois aimed at polishing the process to a finer, brighter, more beneficent sheen.

In readying this scholarly and profound final chapter, the author has invested years of exhaustive, painstaking research into man's efforts to live in peace. His knowledge of the subject and his qualifications are readily apparent.

In his opening remarks, he notes the impressive historical achievements of the most outstanding rulers of all time. The good that has been developed for eternity through the political method is set down in such a way that the conclusion is blatantly obvious. Of particular significance is the factual, irrefutable evidence he offers to demonstrate the superiority of constitutional government as opposed to other forms of totalitarianism and the ancient slave/slavemaster relationship.

For those who steadfastly hold to the notion that political methods and limited, controlled violence in the hands of reliable people provide the only way to live in a civilized, productive society, charts and graphs with accompanying statistical data display objective evidence of the kind rarely found in today's world of pedantry. To disagree with the author past this point would indicate ut-

None of the Above ☑

ter naiveté, a closed mind, or a dogmatism beyond comprehension.

But this exhaustive study goes even further. It points up with dramatic emphasis the effectiveness of the entire system of justice that is practiced by the free nations today.

It is amazing that such depth has been reached in a single, condensed chapter. The author has displayed a unique literary style which is, in itself, worthy of particular praise. His use of the written word is at once orderly, rigorously logical and lyrical. It carries the reader into the outer reaches of the cosmos that heretofore have been touched only by a select few, gifted men of wisdom.

The reader will find himself completing the chapter so quickly it will appear that he has merely been flipping blank pages. However, upon completion he will experience the quiet satisfaction one enjoys as a result of a deeply satisfying, richly rewarding glimpse of the crystalline essence of truth.

This succinct chapter is required reading, especially for politicians and economists. While savoring the content, the reader will think of many persons who could profit from these insights.

To refute irrevocably the spurious, idealistic notion that men can be free only in a society *without* political protection, the author draws on the combined knowledge of political scientists, poli-

None of the Above ☑

ticians, elected officials, economists, philosophers and businessmen, and finally, elucidates the best arguments and supports them with empirical evidence. This chapter, although brief, will stand as the definitive reference in its field. It combines all the reasons for supporting political action, governmental controls and the "just" power of the state. To understand all that is in this chapter is to understand everything of value in the process of politics and the use of violence.

Sit back then, and enjoy this stimulating and engrossing presentation of the case for political action.

About the Author

SY LEON has been a business and marketing consultant and is presently active in the financial service community. He took some time out from the business world in the 60s and 70s and was an instructor and administrator with a private educational institution.

People who have known him since his childhood in Chicago will readily agree that he has been one who was not easily influenced or controlled by others. His deeply held insistence that each person has an inalienable right to make their own choices and not to interfere with any others seems to have genetic roots and has led him to study, write and advocate the doctrine of the classic liberal/libertarian view.

Leon is the founder of the movement to amend the political ballot to include the option "None of the Above is Acceptable." He believes this would provide the opportunity for those who do not want to cast a "negative" vote for the Lesser of Two Evils to participate, and to have their vote counted as a true expression of their view.

Sy is not aligned philosophically or actively with any political party or candidate, believing that real constructive change in how we view politics can only come out of the private sector.